Praise for *Abso*

'A seductive read; it is at once intelligent, eloquent, inspiring and deeply enjoyable.'
– JILL BADONSKY, author of *The Muse Is In: An Owner's Manual to Your Creativity*

'An incredible combination of inspiration and practical advice from someone who is living the process.'
– ROB SYMINGTON, Co-founder, Escape the City

'I wish I had Stephanie's book in my hand when I started navigating the uncertain path of entrepreneurship.'
– SHANNON WHITEHEAD, Co-founder, {r}evolution apparel, and sustainable apparel consultant

'Sometimes we forget that our lives are precious and need to be lived – every single day – with purpose. Holland reminds us that we only have right now to make our lives extraordinary.'
– ALISON TURNER, Editor, Australian Yoga Journal

Absolutely on Purpose

A Kick-Ass Guide to Unfurling Your Brilliance Across the Universe

Stephanie Holland

PURPLE MOOR PRESS

Absolutely on Purpose - A Kick-Ass Guide to Unfurling Your Brilliance Across the Universe

Stephanie Holland

Copy-editor: Anna Spargo-Ryan

Proofreader: Loulou Brown

Design, Layout, and Typesetting: Alexander Becker

Cover Designer: Jason Botkin

Published in the United Kingdom by Purple Moor Press.

Version 1.0

ISBN-13: 978-1493726257
ISBN-10: 1493726250

Contents

THE WORKBOOKS

AND FINALLY

First Foreword

The reason for this book is simple. I wanted to create and share a collection of visionary common sense for life, art and entrepreneurship.

My mission is threefold: **to celebrate** the work of a group of passionate visionaries who demonstrate the effects of following your passion, purpose and vision; **to inspire** you to follow yours; and **to support** those whose vision it is to inspire social change.

I hope these juicy morsels of wisdom help you to align your burning ambitions and day-to-day tasks with a new sense of personal purpose.

As any sensible writer does when beginning a new project, I bounced the idea around amongst trusted friends. My favourite response was from Diana:

I think insights from people who know and feel passionate about a subject are always quite fascinating. As long as they do not become 'up your bum' navel-gazing reflections of a successful life, but rather honest retellings of a person's experience and observations in a particular area.

The result is this: not simply honest but also raw and generous retellings of people's experiences and observations. Their only motivation for contributing is to share what has helped them achieve success in their life, art and entrepreneurial pursuits, and also to inspire you to follow your own passion, purpose and vision. Definitely no 'up your bum' navel gazing reflections.

In addition to sharing these nuggets with you, 30 per cent of the profits will go to three contributor projects that inspire social change. Krama Yoga[1] enables a transformation of self-image for young Cambodians who are breaking free from cycles of poverty and abuse. Yogabeats Conflict[2] delivers the transformational benefits of yoga into the heart of communities affected by war. Special Yoga Ltd[3] is dedicated to helping special needs children explore their ultimate potential through the therapeutic practice of yoga. You can find out more about these projects at their websites.

Second Foreword

The original subtitle for the project was: 'Visionary Common Sense for Life, Art and Entrepreneurship'. This would have been the 'does what it says on the tin' approach. I was certain that in choosing between the two, 'unfurling your brilliance across the universe' better hinted at the book's philosophical DNA: expansion, space and limitless possibility.

What I liked about the original was the tease factor in the blazing oxymoron and the clearly defined breadth of application. I believe that life, art and entrepreneurship are inextricably linked: success in all three requires passion, purpose and vision. In mastering the subtle aspects and forces at play in our lives we can discover our inner artist and entrepreneur, and a brilliant human.

Maybe, right now, you are sitting at your desk, imagining a more fulfilling life. Maybe you already know what that looks like. Maybe you just know how it feels or how it sounds. Maybe you want to unleash your inner artist, turn a photography hobby into a gleaming studio, or perhaps you have a dozen brilliant ideas about how to transform the way we live.

I designed this book to inspire your expansion into the 'space' where endless possibility resides. Once you inhabit that space you can unfurl your brilliance across the universe. The size of your universe is up to you.

Absolutely on Purpose

How To Use This Book

Web Links:

I've included dozens of links to other sources because this book is a springboard for other ideas and opportunities; some of them are in the 'Endnotes' at the back of the book so your reading flows without too many links floating around the page.

Reading Strategies:

Fast. If this book has been thrust into your hands by a friend, girlfriend, boyfriend, or partner, or you are pressed for time and want to know how to get to the heart of the matter as soon as possible:

1. Read The Manifesto pg. 15
2. Read 'The Stakes Are High' from Chapter 5: 'Visionary Common Sense' pg. 42
3. Then skip straight to Chapter 6: 'The Workbooks' pg. 145
4. Return to the parts you skipped

Medium. If you are interested in exploring the theoretical framework of *Absolutely on Purpose* and how it manifests through the lives of others before getting into your own practical exploration:

1. Read 'The Manifesto' and Chapters 1 to 4 pg. 15
2. Skip to Chapter 6: 'The Workbooks' pg. 145
3. Return to Chapter 5: 'Visionary Common Sense' pg. 41

Slow. You want it all (juicy morsel by juicy morsel):

You're good to go. Read from start to finish, savouring each bite as you go. Chapter 5 (pg. 41) will immerse you in the hearts and minds of some of the most visionary thinkers of our time.

The Manifesto

Living *Absolutely on Purpose* is one of the biggest challenges of our time. Blinded by a culture of 'bigger, better, faster' and seduced into wanting 'more, more, more', we've become distracted from what matters to us the most, and how to use that awareness to leave an imprint on the heart of humanity.

But now we've chosen the red pill and are waking up. Opening our eyes as if for the first time, we see a world of possibility, community, sustainability and collaboration. As we begin to understand our own role in what really is a brave new world, we learn that personal fulfilment is not something that can be bought. Its key ingredients are passion and purpose, and it is magnified when we figure out how to share these with the world.

Living *Absolutely on Purpose* is a declaration of inner connectedness and interdependence. It's a commitment to unleashing our innate wisdom and forging an authentic relationship with our Self and others. It's about living in line with our true calling, a concept encapsulated by the Sanskrit word *dharma*. It's about living deliberately and with passion, and having a vision so vivid that it propels us forward from one moment to the next. You needn't sacrifice the short term for the long term, or vice versa, because they are inextricably linked. Your ability to inhabit the moment with passion and purpose allows the perfect experience to unfold as your vision manifests.

But what's holding us back from living *Absolutely on Purpose*? How do we change that? And what happens when we do?

We're plugged into *The Matrix* from the moment someone tells us that grass is not pink and cows are not purple. We are each born with a unique way of seeing the world before the system installs a new filter into us, creating armies of people who learn the same things in the same way. Our originality, uniquely coded in our DNA, is buried under the veneer of conformity, and idiosyncrasies that underpin our one-of-a-kind brilliance are glazed over.

Our minds are trapped in patterns, values, and beliefs – instilled by our parents, schools, government, and any number of other institutions and establishments – many of which do not serve us. When we respond to the deep ache within we turn to the self-help industry, which sends us further down the rabbit hole. We continue to sculpt ourselves into what we are not by adopting someone else's formula or blueprint for transformation or success.

But there is another way.

When we become aware of our Self we master a one-of-a-kind blueprint as unique as we are. This is the key to living *Absolutely on Purpose*. When we reject the stories, patterns, values and beliefs that don't serve us (everything that isn't really part of ourselves), we discover the truth of who we are. Our transformation blooms from within us. The search outside of ourselves can now cease.

When we remove the riff-raff from inside and out we can start empty. We can use our innate gifts and talents and act on our inner voice. Our path unfolds and we gather strength and momentum. There is no question that we're going the wrong way because each moment holds the opportunity to check-in with our passion, purpose, and vision – our own inner compass. Life becomes a playful and deliberate act of collaboration and co-creation with our outer world.

When we live *Absolutely on Purpose* we impact on the heart of humanity. Whether we touch only one other soul or start a global movement, our sense of purpose inspires and motivates others. We want to connect with each other and be part of a community, part of something greater than ourselves. When we allow our passion, purpose and vision to guide us, we share the best of ourselves with others to great ripple effect. By living *Absolutely on Purpose* we inspire others to live *Absolutely on Purpose* too. The result? Endless possibilities for you and everyone who comes in contact with you. When we break the rules success follows.

We differentiate ourselves from the average ruffian by breaking the rules with purpose and passion. We reject the status quo organically as we manifest a crystal-clear vision. Our numbers are growing as a secret rebellion stirs at the heart of humanity. As we stir from a deep sleep and gather the confidence to revolutionise the way we live, we look to those who have gone before us for inspiration and guidance. Characterised by individuality rather than conformity, the old paradigm bites the dust as we begin to understand that imitation is certain spiritual suicide. Visionary leaders around the globe are stepping forward to empower others with this message as they show what it's like to live with passion, purpose and vision.

This project brings together the wisdom of forty-nine visionaries from around the world who live with passion and purpose while they make it their life's work to sculpt (and re-sculpt) their vision. They've achieved dizzying heights of establishment-approved success, together with the money and lifestyle that goes with it, and their own success metrics (connection, collaboration and community). They share their insights to inspire your own path, wherever that leads. In their words and stories you will find no judgements or limitations. Instead you will find an unlimited source of encouragement, guidance, advice and strategies to propel you forward in all aspects of your life, including your art or start-up, and the inspiration to define your own passion, purpose and vision.

Beyond their wisdom, 'The Workbooks' put you face to face with your most raw, unapologetic self, and prime you for defining your own passion, purpose and vision (PPV). You are suddenly in possession of the three tools required to unfurl your brilliance across the universe.

Your mind has the capacity to visualise things in such detail that it literally impacts the quantum fields that surround you and permeate you and the universe, thereby altering the people, places, things, ideas and events in your life in order to bring your visions into reality.

– John Demartini, The Seven Secret Treasures audio

In 'The Theory' you'll discover the cultural shifts underpinning the revival of our innate desires to connect, collaborate, create and share our brilliance. You'll also find out why living *Absolutely on Purpose* with passion and vision is on-trend and how these visionaries demonstrate everything we aspire toward. In addition you'll discover the threads of visionary wisdom that are already influencing popular culture (without us even realising).

In 'The Wisdom' you'll be treated to visionary common sense from forty-nine visionaries around the globe, as well as an eclectic mix of stories, poems, and exercises offering inspiration, encouragement, guidance, support and ideas.

In 'The Workbooks' you will get your hands dirty. You will:

- **Evaluate** the importance of going with the flow, living in the moment and stepping out of your comfort zone.

- **Develop** greater awareness around your thoughts, actions, emotions and body, and learn how they affect your success.

- **Integrate** breath, movement, stillness, space, and nature to energise and empower yourself.

- **Learn** the power of being kind, truthful and brave and discover your creative genius and innate talents.

- **Challenge** your core beliefs, values, limitations and judgements, and be able to handle conflict.

- **Discover** new strategies to obliterate 'monkey mind' and find out how to bite the bullet to 'get started'.

- **Brainstorm** your passions, purpose and vision, and play with their perfect expression.

In 'And Finally', you'll discover the inspiration behind this project.

Living *Absolutely on Purpose* is the challenge of a lifetime. You come face to face with not only the system, but your Self. Sure, you can play it safe, but life is not a spectator sport. It's not a game you can win or lose. It's a one-time limited-edition experience that can be magnified by leaning into your edge when you encounter it. To hell with the rules. This a choose-your-own adventure story. It's *your* story.

If you have a soul-deep impulse for change, a burning ambition, a recurring idea, however weird or wacky, or simply want to re-evaluate, hold this desire close to your chest as you read this book. Allow your inner world to come face to face with your outer reality, the one where we are waiting for you to unfurl your brilliance across the universe. The 'red pill' is only the beginning.

What lies behind us and what lies before us are tiny matters, compared to what lies within us.

– Ralph Waldo Emerson, American essayist, lecturer and poet

Chapter 1: Unfurl Your Brilliance

In all the eons of time, amongst trillions of human eggs that have been fertilized and hatched ... there is only one you: microscopically remarkable, positively unrepeatable, original, and beyond compare.

– Danielle LaPorte

Brilliance is a birthright. Liberate your brilliance and share it with the world. It's designed to be unfurled with as much gusto as you can muster. There is no debate. You, dear reader, are brilliant. Are you ready to share it with us?

Like hunting for buried treasure, 'X' marks the sweet spot. It is found where your passions collide with your purpose. From this point – the epicentre – the reason you exist explodes into being as you unfurl your brilliance into the heart of humanity. When the two connect, sparks fly and together they send seismic waves far and wide, their magnitude felt as far as the coordinates of your vision. Oh, the sweet spot!

How to locate it? Begin by asking quality questions. When you ask quality questions your path lights up. Be open, present and honest with your curiosity. The people, places and things you need will then present themselves to light up your way.

Once you're on your way you're not alone. Your tribe is out there, demonstrating their passion, purpose and vision in both simple and extraordinary ways. Real and virtual communities around the world are ready to support you as you unfurl your brilliance across the universe. This is no space-age utopia. This is the magnitude of possibility you enter into when you accept and activate your brilliance.

The marketing world has yet to catch up with our tribal state. It has yet to realise that we cannot be pigeon-holed by age or sex, or even lifestyle. We are the future, the ball is in our court, and it underestimates our full power. Preying on our wants and needs and luring us with social prestige just won't fly any more; we are motivated by more than money. We want to connect with each other and with the world around us. We care about community, environment and sustainability. We let our beliefs and values guide our actions as consumers, and suddenly the meaning behind the products and services we buy is important to us. We rally behind those who use their unique passions, talents and resources to do something that matters by joining their tribes, supporting their vision and spreading the word. And we want what *we* do to matter, too. Unfurling our brilliance connects us to what matters most, and to the people who care about the same things we do.

With ideas spreading as quickly as they are conceived, we can create, lead, join and follow tribes of like-minded people. In doing so we are rediscovering what it's like to be part of a community. We're connecting to others through our quest for purpose and meaning on a global scale. The definition of success is no longer measured according to how wealthy we are, but relates to sustainability, impact and service to others, and is measured on the strength of our connections and contribution. Our ability to deliver on these measures is directly proportionate to our focus on our passions, the strength of our purpose, and the clarity of our vision.

Traditionally, when people mention 'success', they are referring to a benchmark determined by the establishment: meaning, work-for-pay earning oodles of money, and the material possessions and lifestyle that accompany it. But success, in terms of a deeper sense of purpose, or life-calling, is a very individual experience. There is no external benchmark for it, only the opportunity to align with your own inner compass. While your own ideas for success may not relate to those around you, if they propel you from one second to the next with contagious fervour they're exactly right for you. While we look to others for inspiration, it's our own inner compass that is kick-started into action.

A new wave of start-ups, books and digital tribes are fuelling our appetite for a purposeful life. They are showing us the way as we jump off the treadmill in our quest for purpose and meaning. We are hungry for more. We want to live, feel, work and act differently. We want our passions, purpose and vision to filter into every second. We want to be propelled from one moment to the next. We desire to feel connected to other people and for our contribution to have a ripple effect beyond our immediate sphere.

We look to other *meaning makers* for wisdom, to make sense of our own path and potential, and to inspire our search inwards where we can we harness the power of our own passion, purpose and vision.

There is only one incredible you. The question is: are you ready to connect with that part of your Self and then share it with us? Are you ready to unfurl your brilliance across the universe?

Stay on your game and keep going for your dreams. The world needs that special gift that only you have.

– Marie Forleo

Chapter 2: It's About Time

The desire for self-improvement is natural, even if we don't put it into action. We want to look healthier and more attractive, and be more fit. We might start eating more consciously, or working-out, or look into the latest skincare formulations.

It's always been easier to work on the outside. They are the bits we can see. We can benchmark and measure these changes; they happen before our eyes. The return is obvious – to us and to others.

Working on the inside – on who and what we are – is trickier terrain to navigate. This task is invisible; we can't see either the beginning or the end. When we set off down an uncharted path we're confronted with many unknowns, which can be unnerving and maybe even a little scary. And that's without mentioning the taboo of self-help and personal development. If you're seen reading Deepak Chopra you may as well secure a soapbox and scream: 'I am a lost soul flailing in the universe!'

But for some of us, the need for a deeper understanding of ourselves and our role in *The Matrix* is becoming more urgent. We can no longer ignore the deep voice within, whether it's a whisper or an assertive declaration, urging us to figure out what we are doing here. We are acutely aware that we must remove what stands in the way of us doing that (hint: it's not just us that are in the way) and are also aware of how important it is to *start empty* and with a *clean slate*. Luckily, there are three factors reshaping our approach to personal development.

The first is the prevalence of e-readers: Kindles, Nooks, iPads. With our reading material hidden in the latest (*)Speck sleeve, no one is privy to the state of our souls (or, more accurately, our *awareness* of them). Our reading material can be as spiritual or salacious as we choose.

The second is zany book titles – for example, the *Monk Who Sold His Ferrari* or *The Art of Non-Conformity* – that lend the self-help genre some edge whilst appealing to our increasingly anti-establishment sentiments. (*Cool* and *non-conformist* are magnets for social change.)

The last, and perhaps the most pertinent, is the new wave of purpose pioneers, who are transforming the very concept of 'purpose' and its application on its head. It's being packaged and served up on a contemporary plate with applications for life, art, and entrepreneurship that are resonant with popular culture. Popular writers and social commentators like Seth Godin, Scott Belsky and Umair Haque are serving these concepts direct to the business world. Sites like 99u[4] and The Creativity Post[5] are weaving them into strategies to make ideas happen. Others, like Danielle LaPorte[6] and Marie Forleo[7] are dishing up the secrets behind 'making meaning' for personal and entrepreneurial pursuits combined. With the release of the book *Conscious Capitalism* by John Mackey and Rajendra Sisodia, this approach is also filtering up the corporate food chain, giving a big thumbs-up to those who want to act more from their intuitive hearts.

These pioneers are passionate believers in unlocking our spiritual potential, nurturing health and happiness and using our unique talents to impact the heart of humanity. It's no longer perceived as *hippy* or *granola* to go in search of this treasure. On the contrary, it's on trend and available to whatever degree you are ready to explore. The wisdom is out there. It's up to you to apply it in a way that makes sense to you.

I call this *visionary common sense* for life, art and entrepreneurship.

Chapter 3: What is Visionary Common Sense?

Visionary common sense is the ability to share what we 'know' so that others can use this in their everyday life. What we know is knowledge. Wisdom is our capacity to make sense of what we know. As we come to our own conclusions, develop our own understanding, and combine it with our own experience, we develop our own wisdom which we can then share with others.

Knowledge + Independent Thought + Personal Experience = Wisdom

Wisdom, in a sense, tethers us to the past and the present, but when we combine it with imagination we can visualise the future. This is vision.

Wisdom + Imagination = Vision

When we want to share that vision we adopt a common-sense approach – the ability to perceive, understand and judge things in a way that our audience can relate to. I've coined the term *visionary common sense* to bring these two concepts together. It describes the ability to share practical wisdom in a way that inspires others to form a clear vision of their own future. It's not at all an oxymoron.

Wisdom + Imagination + 'Relate-ability' + Inspiration = Visionary Common Sense

The forty-nine contributors to *Absolutely on Purpose* have a few key qualities that give them *visionary common sense* kudos. They demonstrate that:

1. You can live *Absolutely on Purpose* by harnessing any passion that is unique to you.

2. Your potential is unlimited if you follow your own passion, purpose and vision.

3. Variety and diversity can be cultivated within any seemingly homogenous group (or even a saturated market) simply by bringing your passion and purpose to the table.

4. You can affect the lives of others by manifesting your own vision.

5. Unique creative expression can flourish using the same marketing platforms available to everyone else.

6. By creating your own ideas for success, you free yourself to succeed beyond anyone's imagination, including your own.

Whatever your goal – whether you want to create the next line of organic lip balms or a new twist on the electric car; whether you want to raise funds for a nomadic earth-based spiritual community in the jungle or start a green courier start-up in the city; whether you want to find a better way to do what you already do, or start something completely new – what this group of people share is visionary in their common-sense approach to doing anything you love while living *Absolutely on Purpose*.

But who are this group of people?

They are everyday truth-seekers with access to a very special blueprint for personal transformation.

Chapter 4: A Very Special Blueprint

The search for a blueprint for success has spawned an industry rumoured to be worth over $10 billion – and a host of charlatans who will take your money on the promise of achieving success overnight. The visionaries in this book *have* mastered a blueprint, but nothing like that of the charlatans. It's designed around an ancient source of wisdom. It's based on integrity, self-discipline, movement, breath, inner-awareness, focus, contemplation, and inner connectedness. It's called yoga.

If yoga is more than a word to you, you are blessed. However, if the mere mention of yoga curls your toes, or if you have not yet found an inspiring teacher, its magic may seem elusive, and its idea a bit of a joke. Perhaps it has been blemished by celebrity yogis (with attitudes to match), the alleged sex scandals that tarnish the reputation of the Bikram franchise, and studio chains as ubiquitous as Starbucks. If that's how you see yoga, an entire movement agrees with you. *Take Back Yoga*, launched by the Hindu American Foundation (HAF), recoils from what yoga has become: a purely physical practice far removed from its philosophical roots. Breathing (*pranayama*), movement (postures) and contemplation (meditation) we're familiar with, but the other five fundamental elements? Actually, we've already mentioned them: integrity, self-discipline, inner-awareness, focus and inner connectedness.

There's no doubt that these eight elements can breathe fire into your life, your art or your start-up. It's likely that you're already engaging with these elements in some form, but are they integral to your *modus operandi*? By integrating them into your strategy (plan or process) you have an inbuilt mechanism for measuring whether your vision is aligned with your passion and purpose.

Yoga offers a multi-dimensional method for mastering these states of being, but don't think it's a magic bullet. It's the quest for continuous growth and development of these elements that separate those sharing their wisdom with us in this book from those wearing expensive clothing and merely practising postures in a funky studio. The transformative benefits of yoga require discipline, dedication and focus, as well as insatiable curiosity and playfulness.

For Stephen Cope, psychotherapist and yoga teacher, it's about the *jiva mukti* (the fully alive human being). He says in his blog post, 'The Gift: Living a Life of Purpose and Meaning'[8]:

Yogis constantly ask themselves the questions: What does it look like when a human being functions on all cylinders— body, mind, and spirit?

We're not describing a bunch of super humans here – at least, not in the traditional sense.

The yogis in this book are everyday people, truth-seekers, just like you and me. They are aware that anything is possible, and want to keep leaning into their edge, occasionally letting themselves fall off to explore uncharted terrain. They demonstrate what can be achieved in life, art and business when living *Absolutely on Purpose*. They turn out to have one foot planted in the 'real' world as:

1. Savvy business people

2. Inspired entrepreneurs

3. Advocates of conscious business practice

4. Inspirational teachers

5. Talented writers

6. Exceptional community leaders

7. Luminary visionaries

8. Driven campaigners for social change

9. Pioneers in sustainability and environmentalism

10. Innovative thinkers

11. Creative talent that would give any ad executive a run for their money.

We have long looked to the business community for advice about business, to the creative community for advice about creativity, and to self-help gurus and coaches for advice about personal development. But by limiting our search for information to certain niches we may be missing out on untapped and infinite sources of wisdom in other areas. I propose yoga as one of those areas.

The path of the yogi is not without challenge or pain (their blood is red, too), and they eat chocolate, drink wine and dance at full moon parties (maybe even recovering with a BLT). Their approach to life differs in how they use the elements of yoga to move beyond challenges and maximise their potential. The stories of transformation in their contributions paint a colourful canvas, leaving no experience unmet. They range from stripping and cocaine addiction to founding an earth-based spiritual community (see Gaia pg. 66); from a radio journalism career to using yoga to drown out the noise of war (see David Sye pg. 57); turning a passion for surfing into an ecological surf and yoga retreat (see Lawrence Quirk pg. 70), and integrating yogic principles into a 'conscious' clothing line (see Jyoti Morningstar pg. 92).

They will all tell you this: the path is a winding road (sometimes dark and often long), and your vision is a living, breathing idea of the future that evolves as your passion and purpose do. Like perfecting any yoga pose, success requires you to keep showing up, it is hoped, with a smile on your face. For this reason yoga is finding its way into the heart of people and business alike.

As yoga begins to demonstrate its capacity to solve business problems and promote creativity, innovation and invention through start-ups like BrandYoga[9] and creative marketing consultants like Jen Posner[10], it actively narrows the gap between the yoga mat and real life. More integrated into mainstream culture than you might think, it is found in new business models ('one-for-one'), leadership paradigms (Virgin, Apple), celebrity quotes and literature, corporate culture (from yoga classes to community outreach) and entrepreneurial strategies.

There are three concepts in particular that you might recognise:

- **Finding your true calling:** living with purpose and intention.

- **Cultivating space:** the place from which creativity blossoms.

- **Conscious business:** the idea of business as a force for social good.

New Leadership Paradigms

A new breed of leadership is cutting through corporate hierarchies and empowering everyone to be part of the culture of change and innovation. Richard Branson, Steve Jobs, Marie Forleo, Tim Ferriss, Chris Guillebeau and Danielle LaPorte, to name but a few, have key qualities that give them leadership kudos:

1. They shine a light on what is already there, bright enough for others to see it.

2. They share the limelight with others, and celebrate individual and collective success.

3. They share a vivid vision, which others can see with perfect clarity.

4. They ensure everyone has everything needed to help manifest that vision.

5. They provide support and inspiration to navigate uncharted terrain.

6. They inspire and empower others to adopt a change-agent perspective.

Find Your True Calling

Although some consider the quest for purpose a 'new age' thing, the concept is actually embodied in the Sanskrit word *dharma*. Although very difficult to translate into English, *dharma* is essentially your *raison d'être*. The root word – *dhr* – means 'to sustain', implying that it's a consistent quality that cannot be removed or taken away. It exists as a matter of fact, a birthright alongside your brilliance.

This takes the heat off a little; we don't have to invent it, just recognise it.

Completely unique to each one of us, and implying a sense of deliberateness rather than chance, *dharma* has three aspects:

1. Being true to yourself.

2. Finding out what's important to you.

3. Using both of these to impact on the heart of humanity.

Your truth, that is, what matters most to you, and using this to help others, creates a seismic shift in your life experience, and you realise your *raison d'être*.

But these three aspects can be elusive. How do we cultivate the ability to be kind and true to ourselves given the high expectations placed on us from outside and while also being distracted by all the 'stuff'? How do we know what's really important to us when we're too busy to even think about it? How do we think about our contribution to others beyond our own needs when we have rent to pay or children to look after?

We can master these three aspects by creating more space and discovering the place from which our inner voice speaks.

We're about to learn how to do exactly that.

In strict yogic terms, *dharma* means 'purpose' in the sense of enabling us to serve the Divine (God, Universe, the Whole, etc.), and describes a more selfless purpose that aids our spiritual pathway towards *dharana*, meaning 'concentration of the mind' and eventually enlightenment. In this book I've focused on achieving fulfilment through harnessing our innate gifts and talents that enable our impact to extend beyond our own personal gain.

Cultivate Creative Space

CEO Scott Belsky, author of *Making Ideas Happen*, describes creative space, or the 'creative pause', as the seed of breakthrough ah-ha! moments. In a blog post[11] he describes the lack of creative space as the 'extinction of deep thinking' and claims we are losing these sacred spaces. Immersed in the web, and busier than ever before, these moments are becoming rare and are on the verge of extinction.

Chapter 4: A Very Special Blueprint

Less space = fewer ideas

Fewer ideas = less creativity / invention / innovation

Yogis create space through physical postures and breathing exercises, plugging them into deep thought and giving them VIP access to these ah-ha moments. Their worldly accomplishment and spiritual pursuits reflect this idea of sacred space. Among the purists, creating space through meditation allows them to remove attachments to the Self and ego in order to connect to pure consciousness, rather than to inspire individual greatness. However, I love the real world impact that these yogis have (even if it's a by-product of a grander, more spiritual purpose), and want to share more of how they're achieving it with you.

But first, what is 'space'?

'Space' is a special moment that allows the voice of the deep Self to speak. This moment is created through complete absorption in the moment itself, a space beyond time and mind. By ridding the mind of all its conditioned thoughts (worries, fears, anxieties, to-do lists and general busy-ness), the cosmic, or universal, mind can begin to open and express itself. Think of people you admire in the area of creative arts (actors, musicians, artists); it's as if they are channelling their brilliance from some other source. They are. This source is infinite and universal. Listening to the voice of the deep self is a virtual tapping in to a creative source that is available to us all.

According to the chakra system – the energy centres in our body – space resides in the fifth chakra, located in our throat, which represents *creative expression* or *communication*. The degree of space you create, or the 'spaciousness' in the different areas in your life, is directly proportionate to your ability to express yourself and communicate with others. These happen to be two cornerstone abilities of the most successful people on the planet. Think: Steve Jobs. Marissa Meyer. Richard Branson. Arianna Huffington. Martin Luther King. Oprah

Winfrey. Bill Gates. Lady Gaga. They have powerful 'voices' that move millions.

How do we cultivate more space? Three key ways that yogis cultivate space are focusing on attention, breath and stillness.

Attention

Our energy flows where our attention goes, and it's this flow of energy that frees creative potential. When our attention is drawn to the spaciousness in the body and the breath, our mind is effortlessly receptive to inspiration, creation and innovation. The traditional goal of Hatha yoga was to help remove physical, mental and emotional impurities through the practice of *asana* (postures) and *pranayama* (breathing exercises), so that the experience of stillness (meditation) could be enhanced. Once clean and clear, we can achieve the most meditative, or receptive, state.

Breath

Breath is the most basic form of our awareness of this energy. You could say it's the perfect blend of attention and energy, because this energy (*prana*) is the vital life force that we take in via the breath. Cultivating an awareness of the way we breathe – paying attention to the space between the inhale and the exhale – is the first step in recognising this space. Many practices of breath work (*pranayama*) look to expand this space through specific exercises in breath control.

Stillness

Stillness is the expansion of this space achieved through *pranayama*, the practice of which is known as meditation. If the idea of meditation terrifies or frustrates the bejesus out of you, imagine this: what could occur in the space liberated from mental chatter – monkey mind – if it couldn't hijack your attention? Patañjali, author of the Yoga Sūtras (a collection of 196 maxims considered the foundational text of yoga) refers to this as *Yogash Chitti Vritti Nerodah*, the stillness and clarity of mind experienced when we remove the trash – everything that isn't an aspect of our *true* Self – labels, titles, stories, thoughts, 'stuff', etc. What's left after you remove the trash? Space. What does that space represent?

Your answer: ....

My answer: Unlimited capacity for creativity!

Meditation is simply a state of mindful non-doing. By trusting the art of non-doing we allow for the synergy of our physical, mental, emotional and spiritual capacities – a cosmic fusion through which our potential is limitless.

Simple as 1-2-3:

1. Pay attention to the breath.
2. Notice the natural space between the inhale and exhale.
3. Expand that space to allow creative thought to flourish.

I failed my way to success

– Thomas Edison

A New Way of Looking at Success and Failure

The breath also shows us the cyclical nature of things, changing the way that success and failure is perceived. The inhale and exhale, and their endless relationship of one surrendering to the other, is a lesson in accepting both the beginning and the end as two sides of the same coin. If we substitute 'beginning' and 'end' with the words 'success' and 'failure', we can begin to accept failure as a natural and inevitable element of the process of creation. We learn that failure is integral to creation and can be looped back into the cycle of creation to amplify success. We can welcome failure so that it doesn't hijack our *space*.

So Why the Need for *downward dog, monkey god* and *dancer* Poses?

When you have any pain or tightness in your body, you can't think straight, so stillness of the mind is impossible. Yogis work at the level of the body first to create flexibility, softness and strength – hence all the simple and wonderfully bizarre postures they can find themselves in. This opens the yogi to the more subtle movement of energy flow in the body – like blood flow, heart rate or the nervous system.

Awareness of our physical body builds naturally into an awareness of our subtle energy body (the chakra system that we mentioned before), when the mind becomes more flexible and – yogis would argue – more pure. An open mind like this can foster stillness and cultivate space. Yoga does not have a monopoly on the cultivation of stillness; far from it. When we do what we love we become immersed in spiritual stillness that fosters creativity regardless of the activity.

Your mission, should you choose to accept it, is to create more space. (More on how to do that later.) Then you too can tap into that infinite supply of endless possibility.

Do Good Things

The principle of *karma* yoga has taken the start-up community by storm. One of yoga's four paths to realisation, *karma* yoga cultivates awareness through service to others. The specific definition I'm working with for the purpose of the book is:

*Charitable acts towards others done with meditative aware-
ness and without focusing on the results of those actions.*

Some yogis find the combination of yoga and business an
oxymoron, and perhaps even vulgar. But if money can magnify the impact of your life's work, and that work impacts the
heart of humanity, how can it be a bad thing?

Grassroots start-ups and fresh-faced entrepreneurs are
demonstrating that business can be a force for both econom-
ic and social good simultaneously. Pioneers in this field strive
for a cause greater than themselves; their vision is huge and
their impact is an equal reflection:

- **TOMS** is in the business of changing lives, and is the proto-
  type for the successful one-for-one business model. When
  you buy a pair of shoes from TOMS, another pair gets sent
  to a child in developing countries around the world. They
  have recently expanded into eyewear. Blake Mycoskie has
  chronicled the creation and success of TOMS in his book
  Start Something that Matters.

- **Sseko Designs**, a global online marketplace for beautiful
  sandals with interchangeable fabric straps, began as a way
  to create income for talented young women with high potential in Uganda so that they could continue on to university. Their mission is to end the cycle of poverty and encourage a more equitable society in East Africa.

- **Seamly.co** transform deadstock (fabric left over from mills
  and garment factories, and flawed fabrics that bigger companies won't use) into funky, original clothing for women
  who crave conscientious style. Their start-up is a living,
  breathing statement of, and solution to, all the flaws of the
  garment industry: sweatshops, cotton-farmer suicide rates,
  environmental disasters, chemically-toxic waterways, and
  countless abuses to neighbouring countries and the planet.

- **Escape the City** are dedicated to helping talented profes-
  sionals escape or avoid jobs at big corporations.

- **WE'AR Yoga Clothing** is a collection of conscious clothing and an experiment in what's possible when you design a business around being human, loving the earth and yogic principles.

These are my favourites, but there are many, many more businesses like these sprouting up all over the world. Never before has there been such a strong connection between yoga and business. This is just the tip of the iceberg.

The treasure in yogic philosophy is buried deep, so I've organised a dig. The forty-nine contributions offer a different perspective, and 'The Workbooks' inspire a fresh approach to whatever you're working towards. It does require digging through a lot of 'dirt', sifting a lot of 'sand' through fine filters, and taking detailed snapshots of the 'fragments' of your life. You'll use the treasure you find, large and small, to live *Absolutely on Purpose*.

Chapter 5: Visionary Common Sense

Because clearly we are in this together, though our paths are different.

– Holly Coles

The hunt for *visionary common sense* began in June 2012 and turned into a worldwide adventure to unearth some of the most visionary people in the contemporary yoga space.

Forty-nine of them have joined me in *Absolutely on Purpose* because this project is an extension of their passion, purpose and vision. The sharing of wisdom is an honour and a privilege, and a challenge that they have met with generous hearts.

They are entrepreneurs, innovators, change agents, teachers, writers, leaders, campaigners, storytellers and pioneers inside the yoga community, and in the world at large. Given that our own beliefs, values and experiences are reflected in the advice we share with others, I asked them only one question: 'What would you say to someone to inspire them to follow their own passion, purpose, and vision?' Alongside their wisdom they have shared their passion, purpose, and vision (PPV), and brief snapshots of their life. Their biographies support Marc Holzman's suggestion that, 'sometimes the shortest distance between the two points of bondage and freedom is not a straight line'.

If their words can inspire, propel, motivate or encourage you to explore your own PPV as they did for me, then the intention I had when I wrote this book, both in vision and form, will be fulfilled.

How To Use This Section

- **Fast**: Skim at the speed of light, highlight those quotes that arouse immediate interest, then go back again at your leisure to dig deeper into the ones that resonated at first glance. Bypass the bio sections for now; you can come back to them later.

- **Medium**: Take your time reading each contribution, maybe a couple at a time over a week or two. Make notes as you go, highlight and read the quotes you love over and over again.

- **Slow:** Read one contribution a day for forty-nine days. Read it slowly, savour it, put it down, and let the words percolate. The resonance will arise from the space you create around them.

The Stakes Are High

By Marc Holzman
Ayurveda Enthusiast. Dancer. Hiker. Chocolate Lover.

Mary Oliver's poem 'The Summer Day' has taunted me for years, for it is here that she describes life as wild and precious and then audaciously dares to ask how I will LIVE it. What exactly will I DO with it?

I often turn to this provocative inquiry as a reality check.

Life is *wild*, no doubt. When I look at the trajectory of my own life it has been anything but linear, predictable, or safe.

Life is *precious* – yes, but do we really understand how precious it is, and how high the stakes are? After high school I was accepted into a prestigious university and majored in Accounting and Finance. I have absolutely no idea why I chose this degree other than I was young and had already bought into the American dream: follow the dollar and bow at the altar of Job Security. Upon graduation and sitting for the CPA exam I was rewarded with a plum position at a top accounting firm. I had it all, or so it seemed. The only thing I didn't have was a sense of purpose and deep fulfilment. My individual dream wasn't quite synching up with the American Dream after all.

I have a clear recollection of calling my parents from my corner office in Manhattan (aka The Ivory Tower) and telling them that I wanted to quit the accounting profession and follow my dream of becoming an actor. At age 23 with only two years logged into the corporate world and thousands of dollars invested in my education (and thousands more pending in school loans) this was not an easy call to make, but it set an important precedent for the years that followed: to listen to my heart and choose happiness and freedom over convention and expectations. It took only two miserable years in the wrong profession for me to make a resolution that I have kept to this day: I would never settle for half a life.

Soon after coming out as a closet actor, I burst out of the closet as a gay man. It was the 1980s in New York City, and I watched as an entire generation of young men my age and older succumbed to the AIDS epidemic; lives that were cut too short. I was only in my late twenties, yet I was attending memorial services at the rate of two per week.

The ensuing years were a roller coaster as my career in show business brought me to Los Angeles. Between acting jobs I was also a waiter, a stand-up comedian, a licensed massage therapist ... the list goes on. My loving parents dutifully reminded me that I could always return to the accounting world. For me, this was not an option.

In 2000 I took my first yoga class and something miraculous happened: I felt as if I had finally come home. It was a stunning, most welcome revelation. Two years later, at the ripe old age of 40, I became a yoga teacher. I had always imagined that I would be a teacher in the latter half of my life as I truly feel that sharing knowledge is a noble path. I had the raw material required to be a good teacher, but I lacked something crucial: a body of knowledge about which I felt passionately enough to teach. Of all places I found it on a yoga mat in Santa Monica, California.

In 2007 my life took an unexpected detour: I was diagnosed with a congenital heart disease that required immediate open-heart surgery.

I survived the surgery. My heart now makes a ticking sound due to a mechanical valve that was implanted to replace my own. In the quiet of the night I can hear the tick. In a silent room, others can also hear it. I sound like Tick Tock Croc, the crocodile who swallowed the clock in Peter Pan. The ticking is my ever-present reminder that time is passing and must not be wasted. Because we have only one life, and it is indeed precious.

In 2010, three years after my surgery, I moved to Paris (France, not Texas). I am often asked what prompted me to make such a bold move as I was closing in on 50. The tone of the question often carries the assumption that only twenty-year-olds are permitted to uproot and make such foolhardy life choices. Many times my curious interrogators anticipate a romantic tale, or a conventional response involving a 'career opportunity'.

I moved to Paris because I wanted to. That's it.

Since childhood I've had a fantasy of living part of my life in Paris. It was on my bucket list of things to do before I die. Do you have a bucket list? If not, make one. If you have one, start manifesting. I have a message for the generation behind me:

Life plays an insidious game of tricking us into believing that we have all the time in the world. We don't. I'm light hearted, silly, and relish my sharp wit (stand-up comedy was career #17, remember?). But when it comes to the work required to fall in love with your life and pursue a life of no regrets, I am dead serious. You don't have all the time in the world. Even if you're a child you don't have all the time in the world. Because life is short and precious.

I am writing this essay from my cosy apartment in the 5th arrondissement of Paris.

My ticking heart and I travel throughout Europe fulfilling our *dharma* of spreading yoga to as many people as will listen. I'm not gloating here but rather speaking from a place of utter humility because I wasn't blessed with an easily identifiable talent. I used to envy anyone whose life was directed by a clear singularity of purpose. Mine, in contrast, was a life marked by painful trial and error, and some of those errors were colossal. Most times I was embarrassed by the messy canvas of a life I had painted because I knew that from the outside I was perceived as meandering, irresponsible, and even a lost soul. I was terribly self-conscious of being pegged a dilettante or a quitter.

But you see not all wanderers are lost. Some are simply seekers. I was such a seeker, and I wasn't going to stop until I was a finder. My mission: to find who I was truly meant to be in the world.

Now I stand proudly alongside my wild, precious, messy, multi-coloured canvas. Sometimes the shortest distance between the two points of bondage and freedom is NOT a straight line.

Listen to what the Universe is asking of you. You may have your own aspirations, but don't forget to synch it up with what may be a bigger invitation. There are messages and miracles happening all the time. Are you listening? Are y awake? Are all cylinders functioning – body, mind, and spirit? What is your message to the world?

What are you waiting for? Are you saying YES often enough? I sincerely hope so.

And for God's sake, grab a brush and paint a wild and messy canvas.

- **Passion:** To live life fully.

- **Purpose:** To inspire people to fall in love with their lives.

- **Vision:** Planetary upliftment.

Marc Holzman discovered yoga in Bryan Kest's class in Santa Monica, California, in 2002. With a Bachelor of Science in accounting he mixed life as a CPA with acting, stand-up comedy and massage therapy for many years. Guerrilla Yogi was born in Paris in 2007, a donation-based community class that anyone can join regardless of financial circumstances. He relishes moving to a new city and creating a life and community from scratch. With a deep desire to touch the life of individuals, he believes that there is no greater achievement than hearing of the transformation inspired by his teaching.

Website: http://marcholzman.com

Have You Traded Your Humanity?

By Richard Holroyd
Teacher. Healer. Massage Therapist. Hedonist.

First of all a disclaimer: yoga teachers are amongst the most opinionated people you will ever meet. If we are lucky we might have a tiny fragment of truth revealed to us that we can share with the world. But it will be a fragment and it will be tiny, and we need to keep that remembrance close at hand. This is my tiny fragment: It's all about the pleasure, you know.

Some mornings, after a class, I sit in a Pret* on London Bridge and watch a wave of humanity pass by outside. Almost exclusively they wear black, dark grey, dark blue. Almost exclusively they stare down – shoulders hunched, hearts locked away. Without exception they rush by, tight of jaw, as if prodded from behind by some invisible cattle rod.

I look at their bodies and I think: these bodies can sing, dance, giggle, cry, smile, and *explode* into the ecstasy of orgasm. But do they any more? And I wonder what it is that is so precious that people have traded so much of their humanity for?

When I teach yoga classes I see pain and fear all of the time – held in people's faces and bodies, and expressed in their movements. Held fast, too, like some prized possession. And yet they stand so close to the opposite of these states – of love and pleasure.

I hear and read all the time about our need to grow: 'We must keep growing', 'GDP is down', 'Manufacturing confidence is low', 'too much regulation will hurt the city'. I completely agree, but the growth is internal. It's a growing *up*, not a growing *out* that we need to do.

Yoga is a practice for adulthood. It's for those who want more from their experience of life. More feeling, more creativity, more enjoyment, more fulfilment – *empowerment.* So it's for the ambitious, the demanding, the unsatisfied – not just the hippies.

The Price? Your fears, anxieties and neuroses: you've got to own them, understand your role in their production, and then burn them on the pyre. Over and over again. What's left?

It's all about the pleasure … But you already know that. You're just looking for it out there instead of *in here*.

- **Passion:** Has been to spend half a lifetime working out what my purpose is.

- **Purpose:** To enable the expression of a strong feminine creative power balanced by the support and compassionate containment of a mature masculinity.

- **Vision:** To create a community based around this new relationship called the Lila – meaning play – and to sit back and see what manifests when we stop copying and start complementing each other again.

Richard Holroyd turned to yoga in 1994 as a method of stress reduction. Captivated by its ability to calm the mind, he would soon spend six years deepening that experience in a Buddhist monastery, a Tibetan centre and an Indian ashram. In 2011 he launched Aerial Yoga London. He was fascinated by the ability of a yoga swing to help people relax deeper into a posture, nurturing a fuller experience of 'being in the now'. Richard continues to develop this style of yoga and teaches people to trust their body's innate intelligence, while living every moment as if it were his last.

Website: http://www.aerialyogalondon.co.uk

*Pret a Manger is a popular sandwich food chain in the UK.

Is Your Ladder Against The Right Wall?

By Raghunath
Ex-Punk. Ex-Monk. Husband. Father of Four. Inversion Ambassador. Detox Junkie. Evolution Assistant. Cacao Consumer. Puranic Storyteller. Reciter of Gita.

There's nothing more sad than a person who has spent a lot of time, energy, resources, and focus becoming successful in a career that they hate.

What goes along with that is a deep inner gnawing of the heart when we feel we are *busy doing nothing*.

We call it climbing a ladder of success, only to realise that when we were at the top of the ladder it was leaning against the wrong wall.

Now what?!

Many choose to stay 'on top', but remain sad and empty. How can they climb down to reposition the ladder on another wall? That would take forever! After all they've invested so much to get to the top of this wall and they are reaping *some* benefits. Thus we get left with a culture that curses Mondays and rejoices in Fridays.

If your work feels like play – then you can work all night and day.

For one who wants to connect to their genuine *dharma*, their spiritual calling, they must do just that. Climb down that ladder. Carefully and thoughtfully scope out the walls. Then climb their way back up. The climb itself becomes joyous.

Their climb also becomes the goal. The race to nowhere is over.

Dharma doesn't mean just 'do what you're good at'. Historically there have been people who were good at leading and have led people to do evil things. When we are connected to our *dharma*, not only are we good at it, and enjoy our work, but everyone we touch benefits, including our Self, as it leads us to our own liberation in this world.

We have *dharma* of this world but we have a *nitya-dharma* as well. This is our ultimate or eternal *dharma* as spirit souls. Our *nitya-dharma* is to give love and serve. Our material propensities scream at us to take, hoard, possess and control. The problem with this path is that we can't possess or control our world. This is a world where everything is on loan to us. We lose it all: our wealth, our property, our family, our material beauty. Our control of our own life is painfully limited. Yes, the material path is a sucker's bet. We all lose. What we *are* qualified to do is to give; to serve; to love. According to the ancient Vedic and yogic texts, the *jiva* or spirit soul is not born to take but rather to give. Nobody can take that desire to give away from me – except me. When we are on our deathbed I'm convinced no one will say: 'Shit! I loved too much!'

When our mind is still, God speaks to us through the heart. Yoga, meditation, chanting, breath work and introspection help us tune into that frequency. For many years we may have done what our parents wanted us to do with our lives. Sometimes we do what our spouse wants, or what society seems acceptable and appropriate. Perhaps we even do what *we* have wanted. But what does Divinity want from us? This I use as my morning prayer on awakening:

'My dear Lord, from this day on I am Yours. How can I serve?'

If we can be really honest in this prayer and our choices, we will never feel that we are *busy doing nothing*. In fact our work and our life will feel very significant.

Don't we all want to have a significant life?

- **Passion:** To sing the glories of my Lord.

- **Purpose:** To give yoga, yoga culture, and kirtan (chanting) to everybody I meet, and to please guru and God.

- **Vision:** To create a centre, or ashram, where students could come and live with me for a week or weekend and learn to reconnect themselves with natural living, natural diet, natural arts, yogic arts, etc. immersed in a natural environment.

Raghunath began practising yoga in NYC in 1987 with Sri Dharma Mittra. Fascinated by Eastern thought throughout his early years, and tired of the pettiness of the music business, this renowned hard core and punk singer-songwriter travelled to India a year later to immerse himself in the country's lifestyle and spirituality. As a celibate monk he would study, meditate, and live the yogic texts for the next six years. Having moved his family to the country so that all four kids could go to a Rudolph Steiner farm school, he now leads a simple life, while traveling all over the world teaching *kirtan* (chanting performed in India's *bhakti* traditions) and retreats.

Website: http://www.raghunath.org

Jump from The Burning Platform

By Skye Phillips
Adrenaline Junkie. Snowboarder. Rock Climber. Dancer. Traveller. Foodie. Avid Formula 1 Fan. Lover of French Bulldogs.

Connect with your purpose and magic happens...

Easier said than done, right?! When I think about purpose or motivation, I think of the metaphor of fire. In my capacity as a researcher, I spent the last eight years working closely with transformation expert Dr Peter Fuda, and looking at how humble human beings transform from ordinary to extraordinary.

I don't mean how we morph into superheroes or stardom. I mean how we unlock our unique potential; how we connect with our higher purpose; and how we use this to make our biggest possible contribution to society.

One of the first things that struck us was that motivation, or fire, was a key component of every transformation.

On one hand, fire can be associated with passion, desire, love, warmth and light. But on the other hand, fire can be associated with intensity, heat, burning, urgency and stress.

There's a very famous story about the 'burning platform for change'. It's about a guy working on an oil rig in the North Sea, who suddenly finds himself amongst a blazing inferno when his platform catches fire. He is faced with the choice of staying on the platform and burning to death, or jumping over a hundred feet into the freezing water below. He jumps. Miraculously, he survives the impact and is rescued by boat shortly before succumbing to hypothermia. When asked why he jumped, he said he chose 'better probable death than certain death'.

We all have burning platforms in our lives. These may be in the form of job pressures, deadlines, health issues, or even just plain old fear of failure. But burning platforms don't motivate us to bring out our best self. They cause fear, anxiety, avoidance and burnout. They cause us to run around with our pants on fire, or, worse still, deliberately lighting fires in order to get things done.

Through our research, Doctor Fuda and I discovered that to live on purpose means shifting from a burning platform to a burning ambition. A burning ambition is a very personal, aspiration-centred motivation that is highly unique to each of us.

It is my belief that all of us of us are inherently perfect bundles of potential, and that ordinary people can achieve extraordinary things. My advice is to look at yourself as a whole person. Each of us has an eclectic mix of experiences, skills, strengths, passions and opportunities. There is a sweet spot in the middle of all of these things, where we can add our highest amount of value. In this sweet spot, we can be on purpose all the time.

This is something I've been experimenting with myself lately. Having spent ten great years in the corporate world, I could have kept travelling down the path that was unfolding for me. But my life took an unexpected turn when I injured myself in yoga, quite badly (I know, it's meant to be *good for us*).

This resulted in a major hip operation, not to mention plenty of pain, regret and forced downtime. I couldn't shake off the feeling that it was setting me back from what I wanted to achieve. But, on the flip side, it was a golden opportunity to hit the pause button on my life and review the footage from behind the scenes.

I looked at how far I had come, and was really proud of what I had achieved. But I realised I was semi-consciously travelling down a path where I was not in charge of my own destiny. I wanted to know where this path was taking me, so I hit the fast forward button on my life. I watched with horror the 'crisis of confidence' scene that unfolded before my eyes. This was closely followed by the 'What's the meaning of my life?' scene! I knew one thing for sure. I wanted to steer clear of the 'If only I'd been brave enough to follow a different path when I was young' scene!

And then it struck me. I wasn't trapped. There was no predetermined ending. Life is a choose-your-own-adventure story, and I was at a key fork in the road.

So what did I do? I embraced my inner child and got out the coloured markers and a giant piece of paper. I literally drew six overlapping circles on my page and listed out my *experiences, skills, strengths, passions* and *opportunities* in the circles. Then I pondered the tiny space in-between where all of the circles intersected ... my sweet spot ... my unique offering to the world.

I realised that I am an established researcher, writer and storyteller, with a passion for understanding how inspirational people tick. I believe that yoga is one of the most powerful vehicles for physical, emotional and spiritual transformation. What's more, I love to travel, and have a wonderful network of yoga connections around the world. Boom – there was my sweet spot!

Cut to the next scene of my life, and I am set to embark on a round-the-world story-writing mission, interviewing as many yogis as I can and writing their stories. It's a big risk, but I have never felt so sure that I am on the right path.

- **Passion:** Connecting with inspirational and authentic people, and taking a deep dive with them to uncover their story.

- **Purpose:** To inspire transformation at three levels: body, mind and soul.

- **Vision:** To create a portal where budding yogis from all around the globe can be exposed to the stories and insights of the most authentic, humble and courageous teachers of our time.

Skye Phillips discovered yoga in an ad agency loft and six months later was in India becoming a yoga teacher. Fascinated by transformation on and off the mat, she has contributed to a ground-breaking study of leaders who catalyse the transformation in others, captured in a feature-length documentary and the book *Leadership Transformed*. Now she's busy with The Modern Yogi Project, a portal where yogis can discover the most authentic, humble and courageous teachers of our time. Her mission is to inspire self-discovery and healing so that anyone can unlock their own spiritual potential.

Website: http://www.themodernyogiproject.com

Drop Your Mask

By Ted Grand
Parent. Husband. Hiker. Surfer. Snowboarder. Golfer. Food
Grower. Vegan Food Enthusiast. Road Tripper.

Following your passion requires a willingness to go against social trends and expectations. Sometimes it's all a trap – the more asleep we are the easier it is to turn a blind eye to intolerance, destruction of the planet, and the dumbing down of our culture.

Be really brave. Wake up, and know that when you follow your heart and drop your mask a deep sense of contentment arises. You know that you're doing things because you really care, not because you are just doing what is expected of you.

When you are bored, tired, indifferent, or practising avoidance, those are cues that you are sleeping and your eyes, brain and heart need opening.

- **Passion:** Parenting, yoga philosophy, social justice and being outside.

- **Purpose:** Being a good parent, husband and steward of the earth.

- **Vision:** Being an old man and looking back with a peaceful heart, and having some good stories for my grandchildren.

Ted Grand discovered yoga in 1993 when, with meditation, it brought him back to the world after endless hours of radical environmentalism. Many years and many thousands of hours of training in yoga therapy and traditional yoga later, Ted created the Moksha yoga sequence to help students create an inspired, intelligent and fun practice. He uses yoga to help people unveil the beauty of their own existence and the awesomeness of their interconnection with nature. He believes that this connection brings peace into people's lives, which leads to gratitude, forgiveness, compassion, healing and celebration.

Website: http://www.mokshayoga.ca

Are You Awake to Your Experience?

By Adriana Cortazzo
Mother. Dreamer. Gardener. Happy Person. Creative Director.

It doesn't interest me if you are a yogi or not. Or what you do for a living or how much you own. I want to know if your happiness is your pursuit in life, and if in every minute of your existence you are awake to your consciousness and filled with excitement for that experience.

The way to happiness is contentment, and the path to contentment is a discipline that requires determination and focus. This thinking is the core thread codified in the *Yoga Sūtras*, an extant wisdom that teaches us about ourselves and how we function as human beings. The message is that true happiness is about being content with this moment right now, regardless of its failure or success.

Can you suspend yourself from attachment to the outcome and just be present to the experience of the moment? This, according to Patañjali, the author of the *Yoga Sūtras*, is the secret to life: live in joy regardless of what happens next. With this attitude, all the wins and losses and ups and downs can never override joy. Instead it fuels the potential to live a fully aware and rich life where all is possible.

How do you find contentment? Sit still, breathe long, and look deep within, for only you can ever truly know the answer to perpetual happiness.

- **Passion:** I am passionate about yoga decreasing the divide between my truth and the world around me. Each and every moment contains unlimited potential with unlimited possibilities of what can be. Love is neither half full nor half empty; it is forever flowing.

- **Purpose:** Honouring our truth is worth being honest!

- **Vision:** To have faith and trust that a life lived in a state where we are missing nothing is the act of experiencing Divine Spirit flowing.

Adriana Cortazzo came to yoga at a time when all she was consumed with was 'ME'. Her first class cost less than a coffee; she felt alive and wanted to know how to hold on to that feeling. Through yoga she conquered Hashimoto's disease, which threatened her energy and fertility. A mother of three, she balances motherhood with her roles as Creative Director of Marie Claire Australia and yoga teacher (the latter of which includes teaching in prison once a week). The founder of *bent people,* seeing a student walk into class in one state and leaving shifted, less compounded and more expansive makes her feel she has served well.

Website: http://bentpeople.com ✳

What if You Dared?

By David Sye
Social Activist. Innovator. Community Leader. Radio journalist.
Peacemaker.

Many summers ago, a man climbed a hill high above the light pollution of the city simply to gaze at the clear night sky.

Lying on his back he stared up into the endless diamond-clustered heavens above.

Until eventually he fell off into an easy sleep.

When finally he awoke. He discovered these strange words. Written upon his heart.

What if you dared drop your addiction to what you define as reality for an addiction to the true truth of truth alone?

What if you dared exchange your addiction for the practice of yoga for an addiction to the practice of life?

What if you dared drop your addiction to religion, cults, gurus, beliefs, fashion and celebrity for an addiction to your own walk through life and its sacred nature above all else?

What if you dared allow yourself to become addicted to the self-observation and nurturing of your personal life and times, completely forgoing the popular 24–7 political soap-opera media-entertainment addiction of your world?

And what if you dared end the tragic addiction and theatre of falling in and out of what you loosely call love for the innate experience of love actually arising by itself?

For itself?

Out of itself?

Within yourself?

Forgoing the popular needs of your species and desire for external enslavement?

And what if your kind could dare end its timeless addiction with fear

And laugh out loud rebelliously, stick one finger up

At that unstable psychotic megalomaniac that your world endlessly bows before and worships?

What if you dared to turn your back on that redundant entity you call God and instead decided to become addicted to the natural joys of simple existence alone, celebrating every sweet second of life?

What if you dared?

What if you dared!

What if you dared.

- **Passion:** Consciousness
- **Purpose:** Consciousness
- **Vision:** Consciousness

David Sye began practising yoga twenty-five years ago after ten sessions of Tibetan yoga eradicated tumours. In 1990 he travelled to Yugoslavia as a radio journalist and found himself caught up in the Bosnian war. He began teaching yoga with music to drown out the noise, and Yogabeats was born. Back in London in 1995, clubbers would queue for his Cuban Rap-inspired classes, and he began supporting community projects with urban youth. Supported by the Dalai Lama, Yoga Beats Conflict aims to resolve conflicts in communities from the UK to the Middle East. He is on a mission to have yoga recognised and used as tool for social change.

Website: http://yogabeats.com ✳

Wake Up to This Moment

By Mark Davies
Cyclist. Rock climber. Mountaineer. Guitarist. Movie lover.
Teacher.

There is no right or wrong way to be in life.

It is not about what you *do*; it's about being present in the moment.

⟨ Each one of us is a perfect experience unfolding. ⟩

Whatever you do at this time, allow yourself to be awake within this experience and be present in your actions. The more awake and present you are, the more you will find joy and contentment in the everyday and the mundane.

The more you are in the moment the more you can discover and accept who you already are and the more your unique vibration will be able to express itself so that you naturally find your purpose.

All negativity and blocks in life stem from not being in the present, so let go of imagination, desire and wanting for a moment, and start with *being*.

- **Passion:** Accessing the inner stillness that comes from being at one with universal love.

- **Purpose:** Through being kind and loving myself, allowing that love to reach others through teaching and guiding.

- **Vision:** To live my life as congruently as possible with love at the core, so that I can help others discover their own inner love and enlightenment.

Mark Davies has been practising yoga since 1994, but his true passion is meditation, which he started intuitively at the age of seven even though he did not know what it was called. He has since experienced many techniques: breath, affirmation, visualisation, crystal, mandala, mantra and *Kundalini*. Since the 1990s he has been practising Pure Energy Meditation. He believes his scientific background (a BSc and MSc in biology) has enabled him to develop an evidence-based teaching style. He focuses on inspiring people to explore their own experience of meditation and give birth to their own realisations.

Website: http://www.pureenergymeditation.com

Step Out of Your Comfort Zone

By Laura Knowles
Kinesiologist. Nutritionist. Lecturer. Director. Tantrica. Explorer.
Dream Creator.

It all fell apart in May 2010.

I woke up and realised I was living in the wrong city, doing the wrong job, married to the wrong man.

My yogic journey began two years before, kicking off an endless introspection of just about everything. The girl I was – marketing exec, commuter, party animal, and atheist – was no longer content with what life was giving her.

I started searching for something. My husband would ask 'why can't you just be happy?' I now know that what I was looking for was *myself,* and I wouldn't rest until I found her.

My first resistance was towards God. I had grown up in a Christian school with hymns, prayers and a big picture of a white bearded man looking down from the clouds in a judgemental fashion. Even from a young age I thought it was all a load of rubbish and I rejected the whole concept.

My yogic journey asked me to unpick all my beliefs, opinions and definition around 'God'. It was difficult at first to get my preconceptions out of the way, but eventually God and I started to have a conversation and our relationship began. This was a path of deepening into myself: I began to feel an energy within me that was connected to everything. This became my definition of God. And not a white beard in sight.

I have never done anything by halves, and in typical style I proceeded to turn my entire life upside down. I left my husband, packed in my job, moved in with my parents and experienced a total unravelling of everything.

Through that turbulent, terrifying year I clung to my daily yoga practice. It was the only place where I felt secure. It gave me a 'constant' in a chaotic world and it was the only place that truly felt like home. I now look back at the emotional rollercoaster I was on and know that my yoga mat held me through it all. I cried, wailed and raged on that mat. It nourished, guided and loved me every step of the way. I will always be so grateful for that.

I rebuilt my life. I retrained in a career that now brings me a ridiculous amount of joy. After two years of single-dom I met a man with a kind heart who was willing to step up, do the work himself and be open to random discussions around spirituality. We are moving to a house by the sea.

My life is unrecognisable from the one I had five years ago, all because I chose to follow my heart and not my head.

Once I step outside my comfort zone I am able to have a real experience of who I really am.

Control is an illusion of the mind to try and keep me safe. Instead it keeps me prisoner. The trick is to let go of the control and discover freedom.

Fall in love with yourself. Become aware of the voice inside your head and listen to what it says. If it's unkind, change it. Talk to yourself like you would a five-year-old child – gentle, warm and loving. Now is the time to acknowledge and celebrate how fabulous you truly are!

The truth is not in the mind but in the body. When my mind becomes stuck I choose to switch it off and move my body and breath. This is where I find all the answers.

"I am always safe at the core of my being" + "I stand in my own personal power"

Attitude creates reality. If I focus on lack I receive lack. If I focus on abundance I receive abundance.

Recognise the other person is you (this is my favourite *Kundalini* Aquarian-age Sutra).

- **Passion**: Taking the journey within.

- **Purpose**: Opening the door for those who want to discover who they truly are.

- **Vision**: Empowering myself and others to reclaim our full potential.

Laura Knowles was introduced to *Kundalini* yoga in 2008 by her best friend. Left shaken and emotional by the very first class, she plunged head first into teacher training to experience more. Passionate about initiating a dialogue with the body to uncover underlying health issues, she co-founded Balanced Wellness, a multi-disciplinary healing centre based in Portsmouth, UK. They apply feminine wisdom to their business, using feeling, intuition and flow as well as intelligence, thought and factual data. She integrates the teaching of *Kundalini* within her business, with her clients in the clinic and as a guide for her own life.

Website: http://www.balancedwellness.co.uk

Accept Who You Are

By Charlotte Carnegie
Tutor. Therapist. Author. Mother. Lawyer. Singer. Pianist. Musical Comedienne.

I have discovered through long experience that for most people, myself included, reading and listening and talking about 'self-improvement' and 'self-help' don't actually make any difference in the long run. With the best of intentions, it's very difficult on your own to do anything but paper over the cracks.

The only thing that actually makes a real difference is to accept – and by that I mean *pay attention to and make space for* (with an open body and mind) – what is actually happening NOW and what you are, and what you think you are, NOW.

People don't like doing that because it's nicer to ignore all the bad stuff and strive (or hope!) for something positive in the future – but then when the enthusiasm wears off, unless you've actually done the work of digging through the dirt and really questioning everything you think about yourself, it rather disappointingly turns out that all the same old crap is still there, and nothing has really changed.

I feel it is really important to state that I can't actually do all of the stuff I talk about. That which I can do, or have done, has mostly been the result of other people helping me to do it – after all, the very reason we can't see the things that are holding us back is because we don't want to see them. It's a tall order to expect to be able to be a mirror to yourself. You'd need *really* long arms for a start. It's important to stress this because it would be dishonest of me to say otherwise, and also because it's important that people don't assume that yoga teachers (or anyone else telling you how to improve yourself or your life) can do everything they aspire to either. The truth is they are usually in the same position as everyone else.

I really wish someone had told me all this very firmly when I started yoga fifteen years ago, instead of telling me to visualise flowers and hum in Sanskrit. The beauty, purpose and passion in life is nothing you can *think* of or read about – it just appears on its own when you realise that everything you might think about it is pretty much just random crap.

Nothing you can think of, or read about, or try to force yourself to be, can do justice to the simple and deeply comfortable experience that is going on all the time.

So if you ask me how to help someone find their passion, purpose and vision, I have no idea about the answer. I don't have an answer for myself, let alone for anyone else. My purpose seems to be generic rather than specific. I am assuming a specific one will appear at some point, but up till now I've just gone with the flow. For better and quite often for worse! But I feel sure something will turn up and that certainty perhaps points more to the question than anything else. I am beginning to suspect that there *is* no answer to that question.

Just pay attention. (The most focused, open, accepting attention that you can.)

Participate.

Relax.

Dance with whatever life chooses to give you.

Be ready, and your passion, purpose and vision will find you.

- **Passion:** Becoming fluent at being alive.
- **Purpose:** Revealing limitations and restrictions and transforming them.
- **Vision:** Wholeness at the level of body, heart and mind.

Charlotte Carnegie discovered yoga in 1992 through local group classes. By 2002 it was a core part of her life. Having trained as a teacher while working part time in the city of London, she is the author of *The Incomplete Guide to Yoga*, and the founder of Boundless Native offering one-to-one yoga and meditation classes in South West London. She specialises in yoga for conception and pregnancy, yoga therapy and health management. A mother of two, she is also an occasional writer. She has come to believe that while yoga isn't the answer to everything, it poses some useful questions.

Website: http://www.boundlessnative.com

This Is A One-Time Limited-Edition Experience

By Gaia
Ecstatic Dancer. Aerial Silks and Acrobatic Artist. Spiritual Community Leader. Building Designer. Cobb Artist. Accountant.

Writing drives me absolutely crazy. Really.

I prefer to dance naked. So right now I'm gonna get naked and dance with you on this paper. I'm sitting here smoking a cigarette. I could get all wrapped up in guilt, but I find it's more fruitful if I forgive myself. I'm writing to inspire you, and to invite you on to this dance floor with me. I inspire me, so maybe I'll share a bit about how I came to this place.

I remember being completely exhausted. Trying to keep up. Comparing myself to others. Trying to live up to an image of who I thought I was supposed to be. For years I just wanted it all to end. I thought of killing myself. I numbed myself with food, shopping, alcohol, cocaine and meth amphetamines. Not everyone needs to do this, but some of us need to go down, all the way down to the bottom, and that's just the way it rolls.

One day I woke up to recognise the simple truth: I was here, in this body, in this life. Ultimately it was my choice, my responsibility to make the best of it. I made a choice to live fully.

This is a one time, limited-edition experience, so why not be fulfilled by the ride?

I got humble, I surrendered myself to the will of the universe. I let go, I trusted; boy, did I trust. In a moment of vulnerability, I accepted my desires and dared to follow my heart. I loved to dance and to be naked. So I danced naked on stages. It set me free. It brought me so much joy, made me feel so much alive and at the same time took me deeper into the addictions.

I needed help, and I asked for it. I started trying new things, looking for things that brought me real fulfilment rather than immediate pleasure. I still loved to dance and be naked. So I learned to get really naked. I mean totally bare, raw and vulnerable, open to all possibilities and realisations. I learned to accept myself and the dance of life, even the horrible bits.

The dance of simply being myself, living a naked, natural life taught me to give myself permission; to follow the little voice inside. I guided myself towards the wisdom of the earth. I have learned to trust and be kind to myself. I learned to shower myself in compassion. And I discovered how to meet others with that same compassion. I learned to be patient, to really give myself the space I needed to find the truth. I found the strength to carry on by opening and daring to trust the truth of love inside.

The simple truth is that you are who you are ... and you can't be anyone other than who you are. Get to know yourself. Radically accept yourself with all your longings, all your strengths, and all your weaknesses. Bathe yourself in permission and compassion. And from that space of ease a great power will arise. A great freedom.

The freedom to DARE. Trust it.

- **Passion:** Living fully, living as if today were my last day alive.
- **Purpose:** To serve the evolution of life and consciousness.
- **Vision:** For love and ongoing transformation and expansion.

Gaia fell in love with yoga after taking a class at a dance studio. Weeks later she was on a month-long training programme. Having graduated with degrees in Economics and Gender and Sexuality Studies, she had worked as a graphic designer and office manager in NYC, later taking up erotic dancing and hard-core partying. Turning to yoga and *Tantra* for healing, she recovered from major crack, cocaine, alcohol and sex addictions. She has since created 'The Tantric Way Series' workshops and continues to inspire others to experience the yogic lifestyle. Co-founder of Inanitah, an earth-based spiritual community in Ometepe, Nicaragua, she's on the cusp of expanding her imprint.

Website: http://www.inanitah.com

Feel Okay in Your Own Skin

By Eddie Ellner
Student. Teacher. Investigative Reporter.

Let's imagine the world has enough visionaries and healers for the moment, and that what she really needs is for each of her human beings to spend time pondering a simple question:

Why am I not doing okay?

How is it that I'm not comfortable inside the truth of my own skin? Are my reference points of success my own, or did I inherit them from people who beneath a thin veneer of superficial success are themselves not really doing okay?

Start with your own body.

Is your experience of your own body free? Do you feel the truth of your body as it is, or are you consumed by ideas about a body that isn't yours?

Is your body free to delight in its own truth? That would seem the most obvious and inalienable right we possess: to feel okay inside the truth of our own skin. If you're not okay with that, chances are everything you do will be compensation for not feeling okay. You may very well do great things, but your own experience of life will always feel lacking.

Job one: Know the truth of yourself. That's true success. Everything else is a pyramid scheme.

- **Passion:** Understanding the root of why one isn't okay.

- **Purpose:** To communicate my understanding to others.

- **Vision:** A world where the first self-reference point and greatest ambition is not to suffer.

Eddie Ellner discovered yoga when he walked into Urban Yoga Workout at Crunch Fitness in New York in 1992. Busy bouncing around the world of promotions, advertising and publishing (and writing for pro-wrestling magazines), it was the first thing aside from romance that gave his life focus. Armed with a new idea of success and the gift of insight, YogaSoup opened its doors with the primary mission of being a kind host to anyone who enters. As YogaSoup's guide and mentor he has learnt that beneath the comfort of our ideas about happiness and success lies a deeper non-transitory truth, and now he lives the question: *Can I invite in reality over and over again as the thing I most want?*

Website: http://yogasoup.com

Be Yourself Completely

By Lawrence Quirk
Surfer. Professional Sailor. Passionate Traveller.

When you connect with your true nature and accept who you are without judging yourself, you are Yourself completely. There is no friction. Things open up and life moves naturally and without pretence.

It attracts the things, people, events and circumstances that are in harmony with you. Even if sometimes it seems wrong, unjust or painful. Either way, your life purpose is always there. However, it takes the time and space to observe your own thoughts and figure out what it is that you're manifesting. You need to:

1. Separate yourself from the subtle, and often relentless, distractions or events that take you further and further from yourself.

2. Understand what you like and don't like being. Disassociate from the latter, and be comfortable with that.

As Shakespeare's Polonius says to Laertes (Hamlet Act 1, Scene 3): 'To thine ownself be true'. When you are true to yourself the power of who you really are begins to surface and:

There is less compromise. Less friction. Less perceived imperfection. Less subconscious erosion of the Self.

Your personal integrity remains intact and, in time, grows. This is self-empowerment that resonates and reverberates like a ripple on the water.

You unwittingly and unknowingly create your destiny as a seed in the mind, and it germinates to thoughts, words, and actions. *Your own destiny.*

In fact we all do it; our destiny is created through the initial and often subconscious mind-state. Through self-inquiry, meditation and non-judgmental observance we understand ourselves better and how our mind affects our destiny. In fact, I believe we always have what we wish for in life. Often we just don't know our subconscious mind well enough to know what it is projecting; that can apply to the negative things as well.

We are the fruit of our thoughts.

I wish you the very best in achieving your life's purpose, while also honouring yourself for who you truly are.

- **Passion:** Surfing, yoga, and revealing my spiritual purpose.

- **Purpose:** To live my life's destiny.

- **Vision:** Living with meaning, offering life substance through creation and service.

Lawrence Quirk discovered yoga in the early 1980s. He was finishing high school on the Gold Coast of Australia while surfing the local breaks. At sixteen he undertook the classic coming-of-age pilgrimage to Indonesia, and was one of the youngest to surf G-Land (Grajagan) back in 1985. This, the world's first true surf camp, would be the inspiration to create Tipi Valley, a surf and yoga camp run in harmony with the land in the Algarve, Portugal. Hooked on tree house living and 8–10ft perfect barrelling lefts, the vision for Tipi Valley grew over a twenty-year period while surfing and travelling the world.

Website: http://www.surfalgarve.com

Search For Your Own Voice

By Deva Premal
Singer. Meditator.

I would encourage all seekers on the spiritual path to search for their own authentic song – one's innate gift.

My experience is that everyone has his or her own special gift and that, once discovered, acknowledged and embraced, life becomes more simple. Then it lifts us up and takes us on its shoulders. Usually these gifts come to light in meditation practice, when the mind takes a back seat and the voice of the heart is prevalent.

I found it difficult to reach true authenticity through teachings, books and words – it arose through the direct experience of the ecstatic silence witnessed in meditation. Through these experiences I have come to accept and love myself as I am.

Meditation is all about encountering one's own inner world and becoming comfortable with it. From here, authenticity arises and from that one's innate gift, one's destiny, becomes obvious. I like to remind myself that, ultimately, it's the love for myself that I share.

- **Passion:** To live a life committed to love, connection, compassion and joy.
- **Purpose:** To share love through the healing power of ancient Indian Sanskrit mantras.
- **Vision:** To continue to serve.

Deva Premal went to her first yoga class aged 11, but it was her parents who introduced her to the spiritual path; they chanted the Gayatri Mantra at her birth in Germany and throughout her childhood. She has studied Shiatsu, Reflexology, Craniosacral Therapy and Massage, but music remains her first love. Together with Miten, their music finds its home in classrooms for the learning disabled, during birth, and as people transition from life to the next plane. Together they receive feedback that their music has changed lives, and she believes that through any one of these messages alone, her life would feel worthwhile.

Website: http://www.devapremalmiten.com

Follow Your Own Calling

By Kia Miller
Nature Lover. Harmonium Player. Chanter.

In the *Bhagavad Gita* it is written that it is better to strive in one's own *dharma* than to succeed in the *dharma* of another. Nothing is ever lost by following one's own *dharma*. But competition in another's *dharma* breeds fear and insecurity.

The key here is to discover your own *dharma* (life purpose), that which inspires you on the deepest level, for if you live your life trying to impress others and not fulfilling what you are here to do, you are likely to feel pain.

Years ago I spent a cold, grey winter in London, depressed and doing what I call *duvet diving* – not getting out of bed. My prize possession that winter was the book *Autobiography of a Yogi* by Paramahansa Yogananda. I was deeply inspired by the book, yet simultaneously feeling what I perceived as the emptiness of my work in modelling. I wanted to be engaged in something worthwhile, but did not know what.

One of my friends said to me: 'If you want to help the world so much why not go right now to the local hospital and volunteer with those who are dying?' The thought of going to the hospital and working with those close to death filled me with dread, and I was down on myself for this reaction. I realised some years later that the issue was simply that this was not a *seva* (a service) that inspired me.

Over time I recognised that the best way for me to serve others was through my passion for yoga, which also felt in line with my spirit. This is a sustainable thing as the more I do it, the more energy I receive and the more people I can help. This to me is the meaning of *dharma*: That which does not seem like work at all, but is the thing you would do even if you did not have to.

We each have unique talents and gifts; it is our duty to utilise them.

How is what we are doing serving our local or global communities?

Is what we are doing sustainable on a personal and global level?

Are we contributing to the kind of world and consciousness that we want to share with our children?

These are important questions as we move into what my teacher calls the Aquarian Age, where we are being asked to change the paradigm of how we think and do business. There is an opportunity for us to recognise and access our true power. Not power that is divisive, or power over another, but a power that recognises that we are all part of the same whole. What we do to another we do to ourselves.

The new paradigm is one of cooperation and collaboration with an abundance consciousness; there is enough for everyone if we take only what we need. True wealth comes from within. True prosperity lies in our ability to overcome any obstacle.

I encourage you to take a moment of time to tune into your own higher consciousness and direct your life from that place.

You cannot and will not fail. May we all be blessed with the courage to overcome obstacles, the will to stay true to what we know is right for us, the kindness to touch every heart, and a clear vision of a life free from suffering for all beings.

- **Passion:** To practise and share the teachings of yoga.

- **Purpose:** To inspire, educate, and elevate as many people as possible about the benefits of yoga so they can reach their fullest potential as human beings.

- **Vision:** A world of people living yoga, connected to their hearts and creative talents. People valuing each other, their communities, and taking time in each day to give thanks.

Kia Miller discovered yoga in a book about beauty by Raquel Welch in her late teens. She would have successful careers as a model and film producer / director before teaching yoga in her thirties. She teaches at the Omega Institute, Esalen, and at Yoga Journal conferences. She is most proud of having created a teacher-training programme that supports each individual in connecting to the deepest part of themselves. Based in Los Angeles, she continues to deepen her own teaching and understanding of the gifts she has to share, with the goal of inspiring and educating others to harness their own.

Website: http://kiamiller.com/radiant-body/

Slow Down. Be Quiet

By Silla Siebert
Mother. Philosopher. Scientist. Lover. Friend. Lifelong Student.

When thinking about what to do and how to live your life, listen very carefully to whether it's your heart or your head talking. How do you feel in your body about those thoughts? What are you hearing your body and mind say? Do you feel at ease or at dis-ease? Because if you are aware of what truly motivates you, what makes you act and feel happier and at ease, you will be better equipped to make truer choices while you live your life.

For live we do, and choose actions we must ... often!

So TRY to know your innermost intentions and values. LISTEN with, and to, your whole body to find out what they are. Let them be your rudder as you sail through your life.

Your life will pass, so live NOW. Know in your heart that you are as valuable, lovable and potentially as lucky as anyone. You were born, you get to die, and that means that you have been given aliveness, a life to live.

Be brave ... deal with your issues sooner rather than later. Ask for help. You cannot solve some problems alone.

Settle with uncertainty. NOT knowing is a big part of life.

I don't believe there is a right choice or a final truth. It is a misconception that life provides you with firm and solid ground. Learn to ride it like a wave.

Really think about where your rational thoughts come from. Which are your own true values, and which do you believe because someone raised, impressed, made, forced or loved you to believe? Do you want to embody these? Do they reflect you?

Slow down. Close your eyes and be quiet.

Prioritise moments of quiet. Listen without fear. From the inside out. Go in.

- **Passion:** To teach yoga and mindfulness meditation, so as to help people feel and truly believe their own intrinsic value and potential. To help people be inspired by themselves and their own lives.

- **Purpose:** This, so they can live their life feeling love, compassion and kindness for themselves. Self-love and acceptance is a must if happiness, kindness and love are to be expressed back to society.

- **Vision:** A world in which actions are based on these values and intentions. A world in which people's instinctual thoughts on encountering another is: 'I wish for this person to be happy also.'

Silla Siebert became a yoga teacher in 2002. Inspired by her own teacher, Lauren Peterson, she fell in love with yoga from the very beginning. She is always happy after a yoga class; she loves to see people feel inspired by their lives and their bodies, believing that the greatest gift is to help people to help themselves. While she was originally dragged kicking and screaming to the open heart of yoga, having come from a very scientific, critical background, she now can't teach any other way. Her yoga brand is fittingly called Yoga by Silla.

Website: http://www.yogabysilla.com

Do Something that Creates Space

By Kate Ellis
Mother. Wife. Nature Lover. Dancer.

I like the idea that any alchemical process happens inside a vessel, and a sturdy one at that. Something strong enough to contain the tremendous amount of energy needed for lasting change. 'Be the change you want to see in the world' only started to make sense for me when I began to build my own vessel, because every cooking process needs a pot or some kind of container.

This is where the guru comes in. In the *yamas* (ethical rules that basically translate into treating others with love, kindness, and respect) and *niyamas* (ethical rules which essentially translate into good spiritual habits) of Patañjali's Yoga Sūtras, *svadhyaya* is the study of the Self, and implies following the wisdom of those who have 'gone before us'. Traditionally in yoga, the relationship with one's guru would be a container; the guru holds the space for the student to become progressively more aware of themselves.

These days we can access this space through relationships with therapists, yoga teachers or the practice of meditation. Having a relationship with someone who has 'gone before us' takes away the pressure of having to create immediate change by ourselves. The relationship – or container – is something consistent. It helps us to tune in, pay attention, and create more space. Greater change can occur when two people make space for your process, so the relationship aspect is really valuable to enable this change to happen.

In my experience, students who make the deepest transformation are those who are curious. They can hold a 'witness' space for themselves whilst we both notice their habit patterns and tendencies. As we age I see our habit patterns – those that are physical as well as mental – become louder and more concrete. These are the little things that we do over and over that contribute and make up our 'script'. The more we ignore them the louder they get.

The work that we do together in yoga is to make space around these tendencies; to notice them until the level of awareness builds sufficiently enough for that pattern to rise up fully out from our subconscious. The level of awareness causes a spontaneous and intelligent shift. It's in this moment that we invariably choose to *do something different*. This is the level at which yoga can work.

When I first started practising yoga my immediate and simple experience was that there is *space* around my thoughts and actions. By noticing this space and being in it, my thoughts and actions became more 'spacious'. This created more time to make choices. I get to choose more.

To become more clear and purposeful, build your passion and identify your purpose. Try this:

1. **Do something consistently that creates space** so that you get to check in with your subconscious bits. So that you get to be more of you – passion builds from there.

2. **Develop a relationship with someone who can help you build and hold the container.** Someone who lets you be what you are and helps you to become aware of the shadow parts. Instead of unconscious enemies, the shadow parts can become conscious allies.

3. **Be patient with your cooking process.** All the ingredients, including the heat of passion, purpose, and clarity of thought and vision take time to cook (prepare).

- **Passion:** Expression of creative spirit.

- **Purpose:** To support others to find, move and express theirs, and to help them build a container for it.

- **Vision:** To bring this to the yoga world and free up some of the long held value systems in yoga which appear to constrict and hinder something of this flow.

Kate Ellis discovered yoga twenty years ago while at art college, in support of the body-based artwork that she was exploring. She relishes helping yoga teachers find confidence in creating meaningful relationships with their students, a practice she calls the Art of Teaching One-to-One, which she has delivered to yoga communities in Sydney and London. Her goal is a transformational alignment system that works with the intelligence of the body, helping the student to create space. Her method questions traditionally held views about alignment; it's kinder, and works in a much more grounded way. A community is building across the UK.

Website: http://kateellisyoga.co.uk

What Makes Sense to You?

By Holly Coles
Performer. Choreographer. Teacher. Counsellor. Writer.

Ultimately, everyone wants a life that makes sense...

What makes sense to you in any given situation doesn't have to be the same thing that would make sense to me. And it's really none of my business how you make sense out of this life. It is not for me to judge you based on choices you make, which make sense from your perspective but perhaps not from mine. Nor is it for me to assume there could be only one way that would make sense to everybody. That would, in fact, be nonsense.

What actually makes sense to you is how I learn. And it's really for me to observe your choices with curiosity rather than assumptions. It is for me to understand that there can in fact be no less than billions of ways to make sense of reality. That would, in fact, be conscience.

There is freedom in space. So I give you the space to enjoy your freedom; to make sense out of life how you will. Because clearly we are in this together, though our paths are different, and I may never truly make sense out of your choices; nor do you need me to. That would, in fact, be presence.

- **Passion:** Human agility – the constant fascination with the body and what it can do.

- **Purpose:** Conquering space – the myriad ways we relate through our individual love for activity.

- **Vision:** Conscious movement – the ability for us to recognise that by understanding our bodies and the space we touch around us, we can understand how we connect to everything else in that space.

Holly Coles found yoga while looking for balance and freedom. Her quest led to extensive study in nutrition, Pilates, Gyrotonics, kinesiology, massage, philosophy, eastern medicine and dance, and took her on adventures around the globe while learning, practising and teaching. A human movement professional, she uses movement to inspire and entertain as a member of performance troops such as Tripsichore Yoga Dance. Dividing her time between Sydney and New York, her yoga is focused on therapeutics and self-care. Movement is her passion, but yoga is her path. She hopes to inspire gratitude for the body we are given.

Website: http://www.hollycoles.com

Listen to Your Innermost Desires

By Naoko Morita
Dancer. Cook. Holistic Health Enthusiast. Arts-Lover.

Doubt, fear and resistance usually accompany dreams and desires. These emotions present themselves when I care about something or someone dearly. When they are around they present a challenge to my dreams and desires, and I have to muster extra effort and dedication to follow through with the latter. Even if I am defeated by these emotions, my dreams and innermost desires come back to me again and again, because they are innate and therefore cannot be repressed. They desire to be listened to and acted upon.

Meditation has been the most helpful tool for developing my awareness around doubt, fear and resistance. Through this platform I have learned to listen to my heart without critical thinking and judgement. As I create more clarity around my innermost desires, I can allow my potential to unfold more easily. In doing so it unfolds with more trust, resilience, and perhaps even more skill. Taking action with a positive attitude also helps.

Listen to your HEART and your innermost desires. To fulfil your dreams you must allow your potential to unfold freely and easily.

- **Passion:** I am passionate about physical movement and creative expression, how I move through the rhythm of life, and teaching others to do the same.
- **Purpose:** To create a healthy and abundant life.
- **Vision:** Developing a sustainable community of inspiration, encouragement and care.

Naoko Morita's first brush with yoga was at the age of 12, not even knowing what it was (she purchased videos that would supposedly help her to grow taller). Later, when introduced to yoga at college, she realised that she'd done it before and it slowly became part of her life. A passion for dance inspired a move from Japan to California for study. After graduation, Naoko moved to New York to perform on stage. Based in NYC, she teaches privately in yoga studios and gyms, inspiring students to do their own teacher training. She writes a blog about positive thinking and living.

Website: http://naokomorita.com

Find Your Happiest Hour

By Racheal Cook
Mama. Wife. Pianist. Photographer. Voracious Reader.
Fresh-Flower Lover.

Find the happiest hour of your day (or week) ... the hour that you look forward to and the one that keeps you going.

THIS is the hour that you are in your bliss.

Things FLOW during that hour.

This is the hour that you feel the MOST like your highest self.

This hour might be on your yoga mat.

It might be creating new recipes.

It might be shaking your booty out with your girls (or guys)!

It could even be that sliver of silence you give yourself each week to journal.

This magic hour is the key to unlocking your passions.

How can you add more of THAT to your life?

- **Passion:** Teaching heart-centred women entrepreneurs to bridge the gap between passion and prosperity while loving every moment of exploring their own authentic business path.
- **Purpose:** Making the world a healthier, wealthier, happier place. More successful heart-centred conscious entrepreneurs = more healthy, happy mums and families.
- **Vision:** To help 10,000 heart-centred *mamapreneurs* share their passion with the world while loving every moment of raising awesome kids.

Racheal Cook's first yoga experience was on VHS in 1999. It was only in 2008 that she realised its full power; the mind-body connection was integral to overcoming anxiety and adrenal fatigue, and it was at that point she resigned from her career as small business consultant to dive headfirst into the yoga community. With strong business credentials, she combines her expertise and passion for yoga through the yogipreneur. She has enabled over five thousand yogis to create prosperity through their passions. She loves helping people step into their zone of genius so that they can bring their brilliance to the world.

Website: http://theyogipreneur.com

Create a Circle of Reality

By Deborah Richmond
Sports Enthusiast. Mountain Biker. Dancer. Traveller. Nature Lover.

First, disconnect from your head and find your centre.

Second, ask: 'What is the single focus and activity that would keep me absolutely fascinated and motivated for the rest of my life?'

This is your sacred dream.

Third, create your own circle of reality:

1. Write down your single focus or activity (your sacred dream).

2. Around it write everything you have a relationship with, i.e. friends, family, partner, food, home, hobbies, sport.

3. Notice what gives energy, what takes energy, and what is neutral in relation to supporting your sacred dream.

4. What changes can you make to enable everything you've listed to support your sacred dream? Some things may need to be removed.

5. Start with the small changes first, then the bigger things will appear small when you get to them.

6. Consistently make little changes in your life to help you manifest your sacred dream.

Fourth, listen to your inner knowing and use the body as a barometer to this knowledge – find bodywork techniques that support your journey and that consistently bring you back to your own truth and power.

- **Passion:** Experiencing and teaching ancient ways of connecting to and reading the body to bring about embodied knowing, intuitive thinking, insights, creativity, and health and wellbeing.
- **Purpose:** Work with business leaders around the world to facilitate human potential through embodied knowledge in the workplace.
- **Vision:** A world where business nourishes individuals, teams and the planet.

Deborah Richmond hit 30 and began to question everything. She had no answers, so began yoga as a way to calm her mind. She has brought all her business and yoga knowledge together through BrandYoga, a platform that bridges the gap between business and yoga. BrandYoga uses yoga principles and philosophy in an innovative way: to help companies explore and realise their own vision. She is also a screenwriter, through which she explores the way we look at ourselves as human beings. Her greatest passion is continuing to explore her own authenticity and vulnerability, while learning to face her fears and form deeper relationships.

Website: http://www.businesshealthconsultancy.com

Do What You Love

By Jessica Robertson
Musician. Swimmer. Reader. Conflict Manager. Hiker. Gardener. Canoeist. Dancer. Bass Flutist.

Do what you love.

How do you know what you love? When you're doing it, it feels easy, fun and fulfilling.

When I started teaching yoga in 2002 as a young Jewish woman, I had uncles and aunts and friends everywhere worrying: 'How on earth are you going to make a living doing that?!' I didn't have an answer, and, somehow, I didn't care. I just kept teaching, even when it meant living with less because I just LOVED it!

After a year of teaching, I had two investors offer to fund a studio – and opening a studio wasn't even my plan: I was just going to teach for a bit before heading back to grad school.

This is a life that only you can live. When you are quiet in your practice, or you're on a walk in nature, think about the thing you love the most. You know that thing you do when you say to yourself: 'I wish THAT could be my job!' That CAN be your job, and the best way for you to give yourself to the world is if that IS your job!

So, power to the passionate – the weirder and wackier the better. Diversity sustains our natural world, and diverse creativity is one of the most powerful gifts we can give as sentient beings. Find your heart and follow it.

PS. The more 'mistakes' the better. Write down your goals and, chances are, there will be at least ten great books on the subject. Read them.

- **Passion:** Living to learn.
- **Purpose:** Creating peace through social and environmental change.
- **Vision:** To use yoga and music in community to serve the earth.

Jessica Robertson discovered yoga sometime in the 1980s through her neighbourhood teacher Baba Hari Das. She worked in the not-for-profit sector for five years, but it is through yoga and music that her passions and talents have flourished. She co-created Moksha Yoga together with Ted Grand, and co-founded the New Leaf Yoga Foundation, composed and recorded two albums for the band *Lila*, and a CD for her solo project *Lost River*, and plays with the Indie band *Little Scream*. She hopes to make the limitless application of yoga accessible to everyone, so that it ripples out in the form of joy, health, fun and peace; essentially all the good stuff!

Website: http://www.mokshayoga.ca

Imagine a World Where Everyone Did What They Loved

By David Keil
Traveller. Teacher. Technology Geek. Writer.

Follow Your Passion

In the beginning I would often ask myself: 'What is the worst-case scenario? What's the worst that could happen? I have an education, I have worked in restaurants ... I can always get a job as a waiter, or a cook, or something. There is always a job out there if I REALLY need it.'

What I have come to realise is that following your passion pays off. If you're going to put all of that time and energy into something, why not put it into something that is yours and will always be yours. The truth is, you might work twice as hard as you would work for someone else. But you'll be happy doing it. You can take a month off if you want to. I often joke that every time I ask my boss for an extra day off, he gives it to me.

Do you have to have passion? Yes.

Do you need to be able to offer something of value? Yes.

Do you have to give that passion and value to someone else so that they can use it to make their business grow? NO, you don't! Don't be fooled, the corporate world is using you and your talents, and I seriously doubt that they care very much for you personally.

My yoga anatomy career unfolded because I followed that which excited me. It is something I never could have trained for specifically. I won't try to fool you. It wasn't always easy. In fact, it was a struggle at times. I used credit cards to build my business. I learned how to design a website, and the first one I put together was made on an old Adobe program called PageMaker.

The internet has changed everything; automation has made it easier than ever before to accomplish amazing things with very little investment capital and little or no overheads. Word spreads quickly when there is someone who is passionate about what they are doing and comfortable doing it. Just imagine how happy a place the world would be if we were all doing something we loved to do?

- **Passion:** To see transformation and change happen through teaching.

- **Purpose:** Helping others to grow, evolve, integrate, and be more clearly and authentically themselves.

- **Vision:** To see more people awaken to their potential.

David Keil discovered yoga through his Tai Chi teacher whom he met while cooking in a natural food restaurant in 1989. A passion for the musculoskeletal system surfaced, and his exploration into the understanding of the human body manifested in Yoganatomy. His teaching combines Kinesiology and Neuromuscular Therapy, and is enjoyed because he can convey complex ideas with ease and uncover patterns of pain and injury. He is well known in the yoga community for his articles on yoga anatomy and is soon to publish a book called *Functional Anatomy of Yoga*. He aims to inspire a deeper practice and the ability to teach with greater knowledge and integrity.

Website: http://www.yoganatomy.com

Turn Your Attention Outwards

By Roman Kouzmenko
Buddhist. Meditator. Traveller.

A deep misunderstanding of the modern world is that outer conditions bring happiness.

Many are preoccupied with amassing the maximum amount of possessions, fame and recognition. The constant search for sensory gratification and fleeting moments of conditioned happiness divides us, and pushes lasting happiness further and further away. As a result we live in the world of 'number ones' and there is little thought and even less action directed towards the wellbeing of others.

Deep satisfaction with one's life comes from how much one benefits others, and not from how much one consumes and how many competitions one wins. Thinking about benefiting others brings real richness into one's life, no matter what one does for a living.

We live in an incredible time, full of limitless possibilities. The system is not broken, but it does reflect our habitual thoughts and behaviours. We have created it. This means we can change it. The way to change the system is to move toward letting go of our own personal selfish tendencies, and act with the wish to benefit others.

- **Passion:** Helping people to become healthy and strong, and live balanced lives.

- **Purpose:** To teach methods on how to bring one's health to an optimum state using physical movement.

- **Vision:** That each individual I work with is empowered with methods for working with and developing more health and wellbeing in their life.

Roman Kouzmenko discovered yoga in 1997 when a good friend roped him into his first class with teacher Tanya Levy. He'd been in a corporate environment since 1991, but 2001 signalled a change in direction when he became an Iyengar yoga teacher. This led to further training in the Yoga Synergy tradition, and then Calligraphy Yoga. Having overcome spinal injuries, he dedicates himself to helping people overcome injury through yoga movement and meditation at Southside Yoga Studio and around the world. Focused on helping others regain health vitality in body and mind, he hopes to reach the level of achievement demonstrated by his own teachers.

Website: http://www.southsideyoga.com.au

May Our Own Efforts Inspire and Uplift

By Elena Brower
Mama. A Closet Singer. A Budding Chef. A Watercolour Painter.
Photographer. Runner. Snowboarder. Ballet Dancer. Swimmer.

Whether it's locating quiet or dissolving traces of negativity, when I'm watching someone else do it I can feel the human connection and resonance of the work:

May I create peace in my family so you can create peace in yours.

May I make enough room in my heart for my truth so you can make space in your heart for yours.

May I learn to dissolve the last traces of anger in my body so you can dissolve yours.

May I hear the quiet in my mind so you can hear the quiet in yours.

Any time I'm near someone who's doing that work, I feel drawn to do it for myself. This is something we can all say — may our own efforts inspire and uplift.

- **Passion:** I love seeing couples, parents, children and families getting closer and more real with each other as a result of our work together.

- **Purpose:** I am here to help people make space in their bodies and their minds. With this space we can see and hold what IS, and choose well how to refine it.

- **Vision:** I envision more honesty, more raw authenticity, and more willingness to listen and receive the truth.

Elena Brower went to her first yoga class at what was then Yoga Zone in midtown Manhattan in 1994. She was smitten with the feeling in her body as a result of that practice. Now founder and co-owner of VIRAYOGA in New York, she's offered large-scale experiences of yoga at venues like the Burning Man festival in Arizona and in front of the Eiffel tower in France, but her true calling is in shifting awareness within the smallest interactions, one family at a time. For her, yoga has cultivated more love and more listening, which has impacted on thousands of families who have been touched by her work.

Website: http://elenabrower.com

What Sphere Of Life Intrigues You?

By Jyoti Morningstar
Designer. Entrepreneur. Adventurer. Reader. Ocean Swimmer.
Dancer. Foodie. Cook. Nature Lover.

Fearlessly consider what is happening in the world (or your family, school or community). What makes you happy and what makes you feel disappointed or frustrated? How can the things that make you feel happy be extended and developed to uplift and transform the things you don't like?

There's no point doing something that doesn't interest you for an abstract goal like money or fame, because even if you have some success in doing that, it still won't bring you satisfaction.

Part of this is understanding the sphere of life that most intrigues you. For example, do you find yourself more interested in what's happening at home or in your local neighbourhood? Or are you more interested in what's happening in your country's capital, perhaps in terms of social policy or fashion trends? Or is it actually at a global level that things get interesting for you? Being honest about what you like and don't like makes it easier to know at what level you will be powerful and effective.

When you work on something you are attracted to, your natural creativity to design, problem solve or manage can emerge, regardless of whether or not it's what is traditionally regarded as a creative industry. It's THIS meeting point of creative expression, problem-solving and being part of the solution that delivers the daily inspiration and the passion to keep making things more amazing than they've ever been before. This is conscious evolution, and every brain and heart on this planet is part of it.

- **Passion:** Loving-kindness! Pure and simple. Love + evolution.

- **Purpose:** To be part of inspiring a loving evolution toward greater abundance and equity.

- **Vision:** There is enough! For everyone and everything. By using good design, intelligent technology and earth-wise processes we can create more abundance and distribute it fairly and compassionately to increase the happiness and wellbeing of all living beings.

Jyoti Morningstar was born to a yogi mother. Surrounded by postures, books, and travel, as a child she had broad exposure to yoga and meditation, adding science and arts (cognitive anthropology and ecological science) at university in her twenties. She began teaching yoga and opened her own urban yoga studio, which at first doubled as her home. For her, yoga is about bringing all aspects of the self and one's environment together, which has culminated in WE'AR Clothing, a collection of conscious clothing, and a business that fuses being human, love for the planet, and yogic principles. She considers this to be the clearest expression of her yoga process.

Website: http://wearyogaclothing.com

Commit To Your Path with Gratitude

By Jemma Rivera
Meditation and Qigong Teacher. Mentor. Actress. Producer.
Presenter. Dancer. Speaker.

Self-Love

I'm of Filipino, Spanish and Indian descent, and we migrated from the Philippines to Australia as a single parent family when I was aged 8. As the only ethnic girl in the community, there was a huge part of me that desperately wanted to be accepted; at school I tried to conform to gain approval and love. Meanwhile, at home, my mother continuously reminded us to work and study hard, to never forget where we came from and to never forget our culture and our heritage; she definitely kept our language and our culture alive for us. Her message to me from a young age was to have self-respect, and to love my uniqueness and inner beauty.

This didn't become a reality for me until I'd spent some years working on myself personally. I learnt to let go of caring what others thought of me; I learnt to love my body, to move it in many different ways, to not judge it or compare it with other women. Self-love is about loving my uniqueness, warts and all; enjoying the power, the beauty, and the essence of my being, and sharing it with others. You have unique talents and gifts that you can share with the world with love and abandonment. As you give yourself permission to shine you are allowing others to do the same.

Commitment

It was my mother's wish that I have a secure profession, so I put my love of performing and dancing aside to become a nurse. I loved caring for people, but had to follow my heart and return to my love of movement. I've always had an incredible amount of creative energy ready to burst out and share itself with the world, so this decision allowed me to have a fulfilling career in something I loved.

I studied dancing, acting, singing, presenting, yoga, meditation, martial arts, qigong, writing, and other teachings that gave me the tools, clarity, confidence, purpose, intuition and passion to continue this journey as a creative and expressive soul.

Listen to the voice on the inside that makes you feel alive and inspired, no matter what others may say. Commit and direct your mind towards your dreams. Surround yourself with inspiring people to help you stay on track. No matter what, your path is yours; devote every moment of your life to improving it.

Gratitude and Responsibility

As a migrant in Australia during the 1970s, my mother taught us to live with gratitude in our heart every day; we were given the opportunity to live in an affluent country and to have a bright and successful future for ourselves.

As I counted my blessings with love and gratitude, I also learnt from her a sense of responsibility for my family in Asia: to assist, educate, inspire, respect and cherish them, especially the elders as they have much to share. It comes naturally to me to want to inspire as many people as possible, to be an agent of change, and to make a difference wherever I can.

Do what you love and love what you do; hold gratitude in your heart every day.

- **Passion:** Creating a new level of mindfulness, purpose, confidence and strength through yoga, Ayurveda, Qigong, Meditation and Holistic Lifestyle Mentoring.

- **Purpose:** To assist mankind to reveal its truth, embrace its essence, and reach its full potential.

- **Vision:** A world full of healthy and happy individuals who are motivated to create a world filled with peace, wisdom and compassion.

Jemma Rivera discovered yoga, Qigong and meditation after being diagnosed with a liver condition. Already a professional dancer and music theatre performer, yoga spoke to every cell in her body. She is fascinated by yoga's ability to help enrich artistic process and creativity, believing in the ability of film, theatre and literature to help shift human consciousness. Her dream is to produce films that inspire, support and elevate. She leads Women's Goddess Circles, has successfully produced her first DVDs, and continues to develop Jing Yoga, a fusion of yoga, Qigong and dance, while travelling to retreats, festivals and conferences globally.

Website: http://www.jinglife.com.au

Be Grateful for Your Gifts

By Rebecca Benenati
Mother. Cook. Party planner. Crafts enthusiast.

I am passionate about the subtle body energy we all live in every day. I want to share and inspire people to look at this gift they have as another way to make choices. I love when I know something in my gut with my intuition, and when I act on it and I'm right, it feels solid, validating and real. I don't mean being right – often I am not – but I love my intuition! It is one of my greatest gifts; it has served me well for many years and I know that it is passed down from the women on both sides of my family tree. I was born to be a healer, a helper, and to be of service to women. I didn't know that to be true for a long time, but now in my forties I KNOW!

I thought I was just good at what I did and was around a lot of nice, complimentary people. I have come to recognise that my intuition is my talent – more so than when teaching a traditional class or giving a massage with the strokes I have learned. I work with what or whoever is right in front of me. Thank God my students are open and trust me enough, so that I can continue to teach or share whatever I am feeling is necessary in the moment. The one thing my students say more consistently than anything else is that I am intuitive. I hear that word and it lights my fire and soothes my soul. I am honoured and grateful for this gift.

- **Passion:** Subtle body energy.

- **Purpose:** Helping people feel ALL their energy.

- **Vision:** Celebrating women.

Rebecca Benenati allowed herself to be dragged to her first yoga class when there seemed to be a space to fill. With a background in gymnastics and a mother who was always standing on her head, she was no stranger to movement and yoga. Later, she became co-owner of City Yoga in LA (sold to YogaWorks in 2013), together with her husband Anthony Benenati. Most proud of her Women in Transition Series, she's created a space for women to talk, share, move, cry, laugh, dance and feel part of something that allows them just to show up and be open. She's a firm believer in showing up, being present, and sharing from a truthful heart.

Stand Confident in What You Have to Offer

By Ashley Gayle Stuhr
Traveller. Runner. Amateur Chef. Ballet Dancer. Teacher. Student of Ayurveda.

It is sad, but it seems that people who step away from the corporate, ladder climbing, 9–5 job are perceived as slackers, underachievers, or, worse, lazy. I would like to refute all of those stereotypes and state that stepping off the beaten path and pursuing a profession you are passionate about can be rewarding and very hard work.

I was in graduate school working on my masters degree in history when something clicked and I knew that I wanted a different lifestyle to that which I was setting myself up for. I knew I did not want to sit behind a desk, work in the cold offices of museum archives, or deal with the politics of finding a job in higher education. Instead I sought a path devoted to truly living and enjoying life. For me that meant teaching yoga, something I believed could positively help people.

I also knew I wanted flexibility within my schedule, and most importantly I wanted to spend my days feeling healthy, vibrant and energised, which I understood would not happen for me if I worked in a traditional work setting. So I looked at my choices. I didn't disregard the traditional work system, but instead decided to focus on my needs as an individual. That's when I began to thrive.

When you begin to make decisions with your head and your heart, doors open and life becomes simpler. No matter what your passion, if you stand confident in what you have to offer, pursue it with diligence and work with integrity, I believe it's impossible not to succeed. I think more often than not folks are scared to put themselves out there. What if they fail? What if no one gets it? Both are valid questions, and both have a simple answer: Who cares?

When I wanted to pursue a career as a yoga teacher rather than utilising my graduate degree, my mum told me that it was my life, and that if I did not respect my dreams then surely I could not expect anyone else to either.

Stand strong in your desire to step outside of the box and people will resonate with your determination.

- **Passion**: Yoga.

- **Purpose:** Teaching yoga.

- **Vision:** To live in a world where folks feel a greater connection with themselves and the world around them. To be surrounded by people with higher levels of consciousness and awareness.

Ashley Gayle Stuhr was hooked after a friend invited her to a yoga class in 2004. She was at college working for the General Assembly of Virginia as a policy analyst, but a few years later she perceived that her true potential would be realised through yoga. Recently completing Dharma Mittra's 500-hour teacher training in NYC, she is also a student of Ayurveda. Teaching yoga has enabled her to develop compassion for others, and an understanding of where they are in their own practice. She lives in Charleston, South Carolina, with her husband, also a yoga teacher.

Ask. Believe. Receive

By Erica Jago
Teacher. Designer. Artist.

Deep down I had a longing to be acknowledged as an empowered teacher, designer and artist. But this coming to consciousness was not without pain. I had private villains of self-hate, anger and blame to face before I could take that leap of faith. It was yoga that gave me the ability to listen and it was design that showed me the voice of inspiration. Practising these passions daily is what helped me to higher ground.

If you have a soul-deep impulse for change, ASK for it.

BELIEVE in your heart that you are capable, deserving and trustworthy of this gift.

Then just sit back and RECEIVE.

This is the truth that creative work offers us.

Art is an act of faith and we practice, practicing it.

— Julia Cameron, author of *The Artist's Way*

- **Passion:** Yoga and design.
- **Purpose:** To arouse spirit and magic in the hearts of millions of people through photography, design, short films and mystical yoga classes.

• **Vision:** Global planetary healing through creative living.

Erica Jago discovered yoga in 2001 while working as a graphic designer. Smitten by her teacher, Amanda Dates, she practised *hatha* and *vinyasa* flow daily. She's always had a passion for exploring spiritual domains, which she has expressed through dance, art, music and athleticism. This, together with her passion for yoga and design, led to a unique partnership with fellow yogi Elena Brower, with whom she has created a book called *Art of Attention: Book One.* The book is now being used by teachers in over thirty-eight countries as a jumping-off point to structure and design their own classes. Her yoga offering can be found at jãgo yoga.

Website: http://www.jagoyoga.com

Be Good to Yourself

By Charley Patton
Traveller. Biker. Hiker. Camper. Entrepreneur.

Gloom and Doom. Glitz and Paparazzi. Politics and Global Strife. At least that's what sells newspapers, television shows and glossy magazines. Consumption of mass media takes away our power ... and leaves us feeling empty and helpless, convincing us that we can't change the world. We can. We will.

When Mother Theresa was asked how to change the world, her reply was simple: one person at a time.

This is the challenge of our age. We each have the power to change, but this power will not be given to you from some external source. Each of us has the power to change, but that change must first come from within. And the irony? It is so EASY to start.

1. **Your body is your temple.** Begin there. Simple things. Start to be more mindful of the food that you put into your body. Candy? Junk food? Processed foods? Sugar? No need to be radical, just become more aware of how much better you feel when you eat less of the above. Read a bit about healthier eating strategies. Consider the benefits of a plant-based diet.

2. **Exercise regularly.** Again, nothing radical. Give your body the benefit of stretching, running, biking, swimming, hiking. Whatever gives you joy and feels good.

3. **Breathe.** Become more conscious of your breath. You can't live without it. Think of your breath as nourishment for every cell in your body. It's true; do so deeply.

4. **Thoughts.** Your brain is a part of your body too. Become more conscious of the thoughts going through your head. Do the positive thoughts outweigh the negative? Be more mindful to affirm to a higher value ... hang out with people who are positive and affirm to a higher good. They are out there.

5. **Follow your bliss.** Don't let society dictate to you what you should or shouldn't do. Do what you feel passionate about. Enjoy it. Pursue it. The rest will follow.

6. **Nature.** Spend time in nature. The earth is an amazing place, with its own natural intelligence. The same intelligence that made you. You are nature. Connect with it. Dance in the rain. Watch a sunset. Gaze at the stars. Climb a mountain. Spend time in the presence of animals. All of it is a part of you, and you are just as much a part of it.

I happen to have the good fortune to live in Bali, Indonesia, and am one of the owners of a community centre called The Yoga Barn. While primarily a yoga studio, we believe there are many paths to self-discovery ... it could be through yoga, dance, meditation, fasting, detox, sound or any number of holistic-healing modalities. We are blessed to have people from all over the world, be they students or teachers, to visit us. It's amazing to witness how deeply people connect, and that issues of race, country, religion, sexual orientation, size, and shape are all inconsequential to our essential interconnectedness.

It's our goal to help people connect with all of the above, starting with self-awareness. What kind of food am I putting into my body? How am I taking care of this life-giving vessel? What kinds of thoughts am I putting in my head? Am I in right-relationship with my family, friends and community? What am I doing to give back to society? Am I making the most of my natural-given talents and gifts?

Note to Self: 'Am I depriving the world of the greatest gift by not doing so?'

- **Passion**: To inspire both myself and others with the awareness that we are all one.

- **Purpose:** To amplify this awareness of one so that all of us make better decisions for the good of the whole.

- **Vision:** To create a community centre where all are invited to experience self-awareness first and a personal plan of action second.

Charley Patton discovered yoga in the 1990s as a way to mitigate the stress of a busy corporate job. Yoga changed his direction; he quit and biked solo around SE Asia for a year, which plastered a permanent smile across his face and signalled his exit from *The Matrix*. A founder of The Yoga Barn in Ubud, Bali, he firmly believes that everyone should be able to live their life to the max. The Yoga Barn is committed to nourishing body, mind, and soul through various yoga and health programmes.

Website: http://www.theyogabarn.com

Act with Kindness

By Lauren Peterson
Mother. Cyclist. Tap Dancer. Actress. Gardener. Cook. Dog Lover.

Be kind, and everything else will take care of itself. Be still and ask to be shown what you need to see.

In the Yoga Sūtras, kindness (*ahimsa*) comes before truthfulness (*satya*). When you propose to speak, follow that order.

Try to say what will benefit others to hear. Do the things that bring you joy. Live your truth from your heart.

If you're not feeling kind, be kind anyway. If you're not feeling grateful, express gratitude anyway. You will attract kindness and much to be grateful for.

We are always changing, things are always changing. Consistent practice over time can create change for the better.

Sometimes, when you're not quite there yet, acting as if you are can create the condition you are seeking.

Life is a journey. It's now. Be present.

- **Passion:** Trying to live in the moment. I love teaching and practising yoga, movement, silence, music, my bike, dancing, the ocean, a good strong cup of coffee, vegan food, movies, Japan and travelling.

- **Purpose:** To try and make the world a little better each day by what I say, do and teach; I trust we can live happy, fulfilled lives if we remember we are complete and can live each moment.

- **Vision:** If we can realise we are all connected, we will want everyone to live well.

Lauren Peterson's first experience of yoga was with a tape in the late 1980s before even setting foot in a yoga studio. Now she's a student of Iyengar Yoga and an advanced (fourth series) Ashtanga practitioner. She has acted in plays and TV commercials, and has been a ballet and jazz dancer. She teaches philosophy alongside asana and helps people manage eating disorders and addictions. Driven by the click of understanding and seeing the little light behind people's eyes when this happens, she believes that we're all on this path together. She teaches classes, workshops and retreats in California, and all over the world under her brand Yoga Companion.

Website: http://www.theyogacompanion.com

Make Peace with Yourself and Others

By Anne-Marie Newland
Ballet and Jazz Dancer. Writer. Sports and Dance Consultant.
Mother.

I am Iraqi.

I am English.

I am a Mother.

I am a Yogi.

How do I reconcile all these aspects of my life?

In 2001 my people were the target of war and still remain largely misunderstood to this day.

I sit here; it's late, and I am really trying to wrench out a bit of my guts for you.

My gut hurts, but not as much as my heart, which has a constant ache. I will never go home to my memories.

Thoughts produce a flood of emotions.

In 1991 and 2001 this is how it was.

I breathe very deeply these days. My breath is heavy and I try to make light of this breath. I find it a little more difficult each day to sigh.

I was six years old when my family was exiled to England.

My mother was English and my father Iraqi of Armenian descent.

We made our escape to England, leaving my dear father alone as a political prisoner.

Your thoughts take you immediately to the right place.

Fear.

My father was returned to us a damaged soul. He was harsh with us all out of the terror we had forgotten him and through the fact he had suffered so much.

How could we ever understand his torment?

How could we ever imagine what he went through or how he survived at all?

As a young girl and then a teenager my relationship with my father was painful; and I had to leave home to escape my feelings of guilt. I kept thinking life was better before he came back.

It is twelve years since the last war, and this time I am truly conscious that I am awake and that the last link with my homeland has been destroyed.

I was born in the Kurdish territory of Kirkuk in the North of Iraq.

Back in 1991 I watched my birthplace being bombed as I sat here in England in a state of fragmented displacement.

I became deranged; my family was still in Baghdad.

I was ill and my mind was on fire. It was at that moment that I realised the immense pain locked inside my body and I wept for a long time.

Suddenly I felt my yoga philosophy had no place in this modern-day setting.

My yearning for the touch of my homeland almost overwhelmed me.

I had to get up and teach my classes each day, trying not to notice that other people seemed unaware of my own personal tragedy and that my people lived in persecution. Each of us has a story after all.

I breathed deeply. I connected to my breath. I stayed focused long enough to take my students into a place of awareness while I held on to the edge of sanity; often crouched on the floor while they sat with eyes closed. It makes me smile now, it really does.

My yoga has always been my salvation, my one place of stillness.

My yoga has saved my life; it has kept me strong and sane.

My yoga is being tested, as is the whole world and all its sacred souls.

I have met yogis who have been arrogant and cruel. This has rocked my commitment, but in the end it is yoga that has saved my life, not the people who practice it.

Peace to all victims.

Peace to all aggressors.

If you are at war with your family, your friends or your children, then you are at war with your Self. Life is short. Believe me.

I pray with all my heart for those who take us to war, whether on the ground or in our minds.

- **Passion:** My four children and my work are my passion. They blend like oil and water, separate but together. They have allowed me to be who I am.

- **Purpose:** I was born to teach. I am on my path and the groove is deep.

- **Vision:** I was born in the desert, so my horizon is wide. I see the oasis and its healing space as well as the work I must do to get there. That begins here at my feet.

Anne-Marie Newland believes that it was yoga that discovered her. In 1976 a book jumped at her off a library shelf, but it was only in 1983 that she took yoga up seriously. Having lived a colourful life in 1970s London (contemporary dancer, choreographer for Virgin Music and drummer for The Clash), she is the founder of Sun Power Yoga, a blend of Hatha, Sivananda and Ashtanga Vinyasa with a dance-like quality. Having found her spiritual path early in life, she loves the honesty it has inspired with her Self and with others.

Website: http://www.sun-power-yoga.co.uk

Anne-Marie was the first yogi to be contacted with the manifesto for the book project, and it was only a matter of moments before she replied with a 'yes'. Those little signs that we listen out for? Her contribution not only touched my heart with its beauty and message, but I took it as a cosmic go-ahead for the project. I knew then that I was *Absolutely on Purpose.*

Follow the Path of Truth

By Katie Manitsas
Mother. Author. Cook. Gardener. Politics and Philosophy Student.

To live a life on 'purpose' means to live by design and to follow the truth of your *dharma*, your personal path in this lifetime, which is different for all of us. The Sanskrit word *dharma* is difficult to translate into one English word. For me there are two teachings which I have tried to follow in my life that have allowed me to live on purpose rather than by default:

1. Be true to yourself. As far as you can, in every moment, in all decisions large and small, be kind and be true to yourself.

2. Work out what is really important to you. Clue: it usually can't be bought with money.

When we get clear on our *dharma* – 'our purpose' – we start to live consciously and with passion. Happiness and the fulfilment of being of service usually follow. If we are not pro-active in our own lives, we might find ourselves falling into all kinds of things we don't actually want to be doing with our time: a job we dislike, an ambition unrealised, and eventually depression.

I think I was very lucky – I have a supportive mother who instilled in me the idea that I could do whatever I wanted, and I also had a strong and free spirit. Instead of going to university I went to India for a few months, began practising yoga and meditation, and stepped on to the path that was my *dharma* to live. I'm still walking that path and loving every day. I consider myself to be very fortunate and very blessed.

You might have to do some soul searching. You might have to take a good long look at your life and figure out the bits that make your heart sing. Those are usually the wholesome and creative areas of life, and the ones in which ultimately you will be most successful.

Don't feel that you have to 'do it all' or 'have it all' (that's another form of greed in itself). Just pick something that you love in which you have talent and get on with it. So many people are disempowered by the inability to make a decision. Living in limbo won't serve you or anyone. Get up and get on with it. If you keep up your movement and meditation practices they will help you become more clear. Good opportunities will come to you if you are open to them, self-confident, and light in spirit.

We divide our lives into workdays and vacations, or days off. Many of us think of work as something that we do to enable us to live, but do not consider it something we like or prefer doing. This is a strange idea, since during the many hours that we spend working we are still alive!

— Sharon Gannon, author of *Yoga and Vegetarianism*

- **Passion:** Education and learning. When we stop learning and engaging with developing ourselves, then our 'practice' is over and we stagnate.

- **Purpose:** Happiness. To find and nurture the happiness innate within myself and then to help others do the same.

- **Vision:** To build a community that supports my passion and purpose, and that helps it to flourish and grow.

Katie Manitsas attended a yoga class in her local village hall one day. That was over twenty years ago when she was only twelve years old and since then yoga has been her vocation. Being the first advanced certified Jivamukti Yoga teacher in Australia, she threw herself into opening the first Jivamukti Yoga Centre in Sydney. She is proud to share her life with a wonderful community of yogis and yoginis – her *satsang* – throwing into the mix just the right balance of cooking, gardening and studies in philosophy at Sydney University.

Website: http://www.jivamuktiyoga.com.au

Truth is One. Paths are Many

By Alex Grant
Digital innovator. Web designer. Ultimate-Frisbee player. Sous Chef. Father. Husband. Farmer. Acupuncturist.

Breathe in, breathe out; make a sound with each breath.

Our bodies are temples and jails for our spirit. Move the energy, move the body. Disease is the result of stagnation. Know where your energy gets stuck and what colour that place is.

Every reaction increases *karma*. Yoga is the stopping of the uncontrolled mind, deluded by wants...

Become aware of yourself. Feel the energy inside from the base of the spine to the top of the head.

The *dao*, the yin and yang, all creation. Utilise your sexual energy. Breathe through Another. Enjoy life.

Always act with awareness. Get out of the way! Link breath and motion.

Unschool yourSelf. Everything is perfect.

There is a reason for what happens.

We are seers of consciousness.

Remove the veils that cover our true nature.

Stick with the heart in all important decisions.

There can be yoga in anything.

Love every moment. Yoga has nothing to do with depriving yourself of anything.

Get rid of your fixed ideas; they are the problem.

All media and entertainment is meant to distract us from who we are.

Truth is one, paths are many.

- **Passion:** Dancing with the Devine Shakti Energy.
- **Purpose:** To bring people together to facilitate sharing of ideas and spirit.
- **Vision:** To help people evolve past conditioning into a place where we are free to be our true selves.

Alex Grant attended his first Hatha yoga class in 1996. A trip to Mysore, India, six years later challenged his understanding of yoga and led him into a dynamic practice that would shape the next five years before forming his own unique style. When he is not helping out at his community acupuncture project or helping to save his daughter's school from bankruptcy, this former sous chef and web designer channels

his yogi energy into FindYoga.com.au, a community that connects students with classes and teachers, and the Byron Spirit
Festival, an event that that invigorates body, mind and soul.

Website: http://www.findyoga.com.au

Your Heart is Wise

By Nikki Belcher
Daughter. Sister. Friend. Lover. Dreamer. Traveller. Nurturer.
Healer. Teacher. Writer. Painter. Dancer. Hiker. Hoola-hooper.
Cook. Chocolate Maker. Surfer.

Ask yourself what makes you come alive, and do that.

Follow the direction of your heart. Trust yourself and the
power of the Universe. Learn to let go of expectations and
conclusions. Truly surrender to the process of the journey,
and allow yourself to feel all of the emotions that you need
to feel along the way without judgment. Remember to express gratitude for what you have and where you have been.

Tell the Universe what you want.

Write it down; speak it to yourself and to those around you.
Surround yourself with positive, like-minded people that inspire you to become a better version of yourself. Don't limit
yourself. Have faith in your power and ability to manifest the
life you wish for.

Dream so big that it scares you.

There is no time like the present. Honour and recognise your
fears. Become a witness to them transforming. Step out of
your comfort zone and embrace the element of surprise.
There is something greater supporting you if you are willing
to trust and surrender to the wisdom of your heart.

- **Passion:** To inspire and be inspired. To be happy. Practising and teaching yoga. Learning, growing and teaching.

- **Purpose:** To heal. To heal myself through self-study and to open the depths of my inner, spiritual body through the exploration of my physical body. To embody mindful awareness in my relationships. To be of service to others. To offer my gift as a teacher.

- **Vision:** To be love. To give love. To receive love. To deeply accept the present moment in order to flow more freely with the Divine rhythm of life.

Nikki Belcher discovered yoga in 2009 when she asked her yogi best friend for a private lesson. As a new yogi with $70 to her name, she moved to Nicaragua to be a travelling yoga teacher. While cutting hair and running chocolate workshops for cash, she was invited to teach a yoga class at Coco Loco; she is now the resident yogi at Surf with Amigas. Nikki loves the element of conquering fear, and is passionate about living intimately and sustainably with nature. She loves organic gardening, food and passionate people, nurturing her curiosity through books, study and holistic healing. She hosts retreats all over the place.

Website: http://fairylounge.com

Invent a Pose

By Isabelle Skasburskis
Innovator. NGO founder. Community Leader. Writer. Student Lawyer.

Invent a pose:

Walking on pavement that perpetually vibrates with the hum of traffic.

Work.

Friendship.

Heartbreak.

A gesture with your hands that explains to someone new how this instant came into being through a series of seemingly unrelated events.

This is what your pose looks like. These are the minutes of your day.

Feel this: Body, Moment, Relationship.

Ask yourself: 'Am I feeling this?' (If the question seems pertinent, you're thinking too much. Try again until the question becomes unnecessary.)

Ask: 'What else can I feel?'

Ask: 'What do I not feel?'

Seek out the dark places and wonder about them.

Let your body answer in a language you are still learning.

Dissolve the pose.

Invent a new pose.

Feel this.

- **Passion:** Unearthing questions, seeking new knowledge, allowing authenticity.
- **Purpose:** To hold a felt appreciation of each person's beauty and strength, and build a relationship with that person on the basis of this knowledge
- **Vision:** I see a world where people are kind because it feels better to be kind, not because of deferred reward or threat; a world where people are aware that respectful relation-

ships are easier than violent ones; that joy is lighter than sorrow; that real love is everywhere: it lasts forever and is never bad.

Isabelle Skasburskis experienced immediate transformation after her mother dragged her to her first yoga class in Hong Kong in 2002. With a degree in Philosophy and Political Science, she had been firmly opposed to eastern philosophy. However within two years of establishing her own practice she had opened a studio in Cambodia: Nataraj Yoga. A local institution in Phnom Penh, it provides classes for the city's expats, and community classes for survivors of human trafficking. She teaches yoga as a tool to manage traumatic stress, evolve personal self-image and redefine the experience of success. 2013 sees her return to the classroom to study law in Melbourne, Australia.

Website: http://www.yogacambodia.com

Awaken. Transform. Collaborate

By Sianna Sherman
Innovator. Storyteller. Community Activator.

Our wounded places are our magic places where all transformation begins.

When I was a teenager my heart was full of pain and my self-image was buried in a garbage heap inside myself. I struggled with eating disorders and painstakingly tried to match up with outer expectations while ignoring the wisdom of my body. These were years of deep wounded-ness, and trying to figure out how to love myself.

I didn't know it at the time, but the very areas I was struggling with would become the fuel for my own growth and the places where I would be able to help other people. Yoga came roaring into my life at the height of my innermost pain and showed me the way to loving myself. As I plunged into the practices of yoga, especially meditation and *asana* (postures), my self-image transformed from one of self-hate to self-love, and I experienced infinite amounts of healing in my heart.

For the past two decades I have been teaching yoga as a way to love oneself. I know first-hand the power of transformation from self-deprecation to self-affirmation. Every human being is naturally beautiful and yoga helps us to reveal this deep soul beauty.

We are meant to collaborate and awaken alongside each other in a wide horizontal embrace.

Many of our habitual ways of being in the world operate on greed, fear and competition. We want to make sure that we get our piece of the pie and believe there is a limited amount of pie. With our erroneous belief we end up grabbing for our piece before the next person can take it. This leads to the vertical path of trying to be on the top and climb the highest ladder to the golden pot of treasure high in the sky. With everyone trying to do this we create more problems and disconnect from each other.

As the heart of the yoga practitioner awakens, however, there is a natural understanding that we are all connected. We are one ecosystem of greatness, and when one part of the ecosystem thrives the whole thrives too. Yoga shifts us from fear-based competition to love-based collaboration where we want each other to flourish and succeed.

As the collective mindset shifts from fear to love, we move from the vertical competition ladder to the horizontal circle of community power where each person is celebrated. This is a new mentality to embrace for many people. In this paradigm, collaboration is encouraged so we can support each other and also challenge each other to be the best that we can be.

Healthy competition is good for the challenge of becoming better at anything we do, but we must learn to source the competitive, playful spirit from love (instead of fear). I remember in my pre-med days how all our examinations were graded on a curve. This meant that some people passed and others continually failed. It was such an anxiety-filled experience standing in the hallway waiting for the grades to be released on a sheet of paper with your identification number next to it. Eventually, I got tired of this, and since I was usually at the top of the grading system I started tutoring other students for free. I would lead an open review session in an empty room the night before an exam and help other students improve their understanding of the material. It was very community-oriented and everyone who came began receiving better grades. We started bonding through the experience and my grades remained impeccable while helping to uplift the experience for others.

This is what I mean by the shift from vertical to horizontal. It's simple: we all become better by helping each other. The path of yoga is the path of awakening. This awakening is a direct realisation from within. It is a true knowing that we are not separate from each other.

- **Passion:** Yoga, healing arts, nature, embodied ritual and mythic consciousness.

- **Purpose:** To serve as a vessel of love, tending my heart fire in remembrance that we all belong to each other.

- **Vision:** Humanity waking up fully. We all collaborate with each other in a wide horizontal embrace where each person is empowered to share their soul medicine for the benefit of all beings.

Sianna Sherman discovered yoga through a book on the subconscious mind in 1989, and by 2008 was cited by *Yoga Jour-*

nal as one of the twenty-one talented teachers shaping the future of yoga. Her practice and teachings weave alignment, therapeutics, potent sequencing, mythology, *Tantra* and the power of these practices with accessibility for everyday transformation. She launched the Manifesto Movement and facilitates Manifesto Movement classes around the world. Open to Grace is the community-driven initiative and the digital platform for Sianna's vision.

Website: http://www.opentograce.com

There Are No Rules

By Jenny Sauer-Klein
Ecstatic Dancer. Writer. Artist. Music Maker. Healer. Creator.
Community Catalyst.

There are no rules. There are only limits you create with your mind.

You are infinitely powerful, creative and magical. The universe conspires to support those who are in complete alignment with their vision and give themselves to it with unwavering passion and dedication.

There is no one way to do it. It has never been done the way that you will do it. You can make a living and a career out of anything, as long as you are committed to it, it brings you joy, and through it you are able to provide something of value to the heart of humanity.

The undiluted energy of being in alignment with yourself and your purpose is so powerful and magnetic. The effect of such a vision is infinitely more powerful the more consciousness is focused upon it. Get people involved; get people on board. A great vision is like love itself; it only grows the more you share it. The more you give it away, the more there is to share.

If you help other people feel ignited by your mission, you can quickly create a wave that continues its own momentum.

Keep the nucleus strong. You are the vision holder and there is no one else who can uphold and cultivate the vision in the same way you can. Your vision is the unique expression of the gift you came here to give. This is by far your most important role.

Trust your first thought; trust what comes through you and to you. Trust every person you meet on your path is there for a divine purpose. Give yourself time to dream, permission to dream, and find pleasure and excitement in the dream. Dream in depth until it is tangible, until you can feel your vision in a way that it is so obvious and clear, almost as though you are watching a movie that has already been filmed, the replay that you get to watch.

Don't get bogged down in the details of the how. Get excited by the now real present opportunity to be a leading edge creator, and take a big enough risk to merit exponential returns. There may be effort, but if you are flowing towards what is best for you and best for all, there will not be a struggle. Seek ease, seek relief, and seek flow.

When you are giving your gift, you are the first one who receives the benefit of it. Make sure to balance giving and receiving as it is of the utmost importance that you keep your own wellbeing in primary position. If you keep yourself happy and healthy you will continue to enjoy watching the vision unfold and blossom. Allow it to change as you change. You are a divine receiver and transmitter. Follow your path through the moments of fear, doubt and exhaustion, and allow your true destiny to unfold in the most perfect and organic of ways. Evolution is a step-by-step process. You don't have to know what happens at the end, just what feels right now in this moment.

• **Passion:** Interpersonal dynamics.

- **Purpose:** Embracing relationship as a spiritual path and catalysing community.

- **Vision:** A world where we have unconditional love and acceptance for each other and ourselves.

Jenny Sauer-Klein was looking for a non-competitive way to enjoy being in her body when she discovered yoga in 1999. Studying to become a musical theatre director, she had been dancing and performing her whole life. She also taught circus arts to children in afterschool programmes and summer camps. The two paths collided when she co-created Acroyoga, now a global movement with an annual festival called Divine Play AcroYoga. Most proud of creating a global family and a tool that helps to tap into our inner child, Acroyoga is anchored in helping people build trust with themselves and each other, and demonstrating the power of community.

Website: http://www.acroyoga.org

Jump. Move. Start Empty

By Anna Laurita
Mother. Wife. Friend. Mosaic Maker. Painter. Mountain trekker.
Paddle boarder. Biker. Swimmer. Horse Rider.

Close Your Eyes and Jump

You're designed to transform. As human beings we are not meant to stay the same. But transformation is not easy; sometimes you have to close your eyes and JUMP. Indecision or anxiety about a transformation (even after doing all the research) can be paralysing. I have always had success in closing my eyes and jumping at that point.

My own transformation has guided me on very different paths. I transformed from a young girl showing American Quarter Horses competitively to a university graduate who had to leave the horses behind. I went on to work for a Fortune 100 company that saw me moving to Hong Kong and then Latin America. Now I own a yoga school and have created my own teacher-training programme. I have three children and a husband, and live in a small beach town in Mexico. I am happy, and I know the transformation does not stop here.

Realising that we are designed for transformation is our first step; this is what propels us forward. Life is a great journey. It is not a destination, somewhere we end up, because we keep on living it along the way. We don't have to wait to live our lives.

Are you looking at an opportunity that terrifies you? If it is not immoral, illegal or downright stupid, just close your eyes and jump! You can't see what's on the other side until you get there, so, if you can't get there with your eyes open, then for goodness sake close them ... and jump.

If you've got the calling, you must listen. I have lived by that philosophy in all the significant transformations in my life and I have never regretted it. Sometimes you just have to feel the transformation first (the closing-the-eyes part). In Sanskrit this is called *bhavana*. It's the developmental stage, when you know a change is coming and you're going to manifest it. If you're feeling a change coming, close your eyes and jump. I promise you won't be sorry.

When You Stop Moving, You Stop Moving

'As you say, Anna, if I stop moving, well, then I stop moving, so of course I'll be here,' say my students when I ask whether they'll come to practice tonight or tomorrow. This saying has propelled me forward through seamless transformation.

It has three aspects:

1. Physiological
2. The principle of inertia

3. Spiritual

Physiologically there is connective tissue called *fascia*. Made of layers of collagen and elastin, it allows the muscles to move freely. When your muscles are stiff due to inactivity (because you've stopped moving) it is because there is something that an anatomy teacher named Gil Hedley calls 'the fuzz'. The 'fuzz' causes the *fascia* to meet resistance. It is a sticky collagen that solidifies the muscles and keeps them from moving in their full and natural range of motion. It occurs as a result of long sessions of inactivity. If we have long periods of inactivity like sleeping, recovering from an injury, or sitting for a long time, we feel we have to get up and stretch. When you keep moving, you keep the fascia clean of 'the fuzz', so you can keep moving.

The principle of inertia, according to Isaac Newton's *First Law of Motion*, says that an object that does not have any external force will move at its current velocity until something or someone causes it to change its speed or direction. If you stop moving (forward on your chosen path or toward where you'd like to see yourself) you are more likely not to move, but if you are continually moving you'll have more facility to keep moving. You can do this by making steps towards improving yourself, igniting characteristics within yourself that lie dormant, and learning more about yourself to be a source of strength for yourself and others.

Spiritually. You most likely already have a guru – this is anybody who helps you to see the light and takes away any kind of darkness. Look at anyone as a worthy guru with something to teach you and you'll keep moving forward. When you start to think that you are alone, when you isolate yourself with narrow ideas and only see one perspective, you may find yourself stuck in old habits and patterns. But when you realise that everybody is worthy and enlightened in some respect (like a guru), you too will be more enlightened and free to keep on moving.

Start Empty

Lose the 'story' and just be here. No preconceived notions, worries, fears or anxieties. I see children do this. When they start something new, they start ready to take on whatever their task brings. They don't harbour grudges, worry about where their next meal will be coming from, or when their next pay check will be. They take each day as it comes, fresh and ready.

I wake in the morning. I start empty. I am not who I was yesterday. I am not the teacher who gave that great class yesterday, and I am not the corporate executive or the mum I was yesterday. I am not the title that other people give me or I have given myself. I'm free to be who I am today. If I tie myself up in all the stories I related to yesterday or to certain actions, then I will be too full to see what matters most. So I start empty. I practice yoga *asana* (postures) and meditate in the mornings to become empty. When something passes through my mind, I don't attach meaning to it. It is what it is. I am simply the observer. The events of the mind have no real substance, no attachment or colouring. This comes from a Buddhist precept called Emptiness. The goal of practising this is to loosen all attachments to views, stories and assumptions, leaving the mind empty of all the greed, anger and delusion, and thus empty of suffering and stress. That way I can make space for my day ahead – there is nothing to get in the way. Nothing that happened yesterday can colour today. My path is new each and every day.

- **Passion:** Inspiring others to look within and to provoke transformation.

- **Purpose:** Teaching others how to look within and take bold steps forward. To be of service to all through my teaching.

- **Vision:** A world where all people are happy and free.

Anna Laurita discovered yoga in Nepal in 1991 and has since gone on to found Davannayoga, the first registered and traditional-style yoga school in Puerto Vallarta, Mexico. With business skills acquired as a PR Manager for a Fortune 100 company, she's created a beautiful sanctuary in the heart of the city. She is inspired by evidence of transformation which she fosters through a new pilot project teaching yoga to children with special needs, and is working on her first book about her yoga style. She gets excited seeing students turn off the judge in their minds and move forward boldly.

Website: http://davannayoga.com

Take a Leap of Faith

By Jennifer Posner (Prema)
Writer. Marketer. Skier. Hiker. Painter. Permaculturalist.

About five years ago I took the enormous leap of faith to leave a life of 'societal security' and booked a one-way ticket to India. I listened to a deep calling from my heart to leave it all and journey on my own to teach yoga and meditation to children in orphanages.

I have been on the road for almost five years now and am currently living in a small town in Peru's Sacred Valley. I continue to share my yoga practice with children and adults, live very simply, and have never been happier.

What began as a three-month journey to India turned into a life-altering adventure in sharing yoga and meditation with children and their families in India and all over South East Asia, Indonesia, Australia, New Zealand and South America. Opportunities present themselves and strangers open their doors to me on a regular basis. These strangers become my 'family' in very short periods of time.

All of this stems from a yoga practice that began about seven years ago. I had always practised meditation and some yoga throughout my life, but it wasn't until I made the commitment to make yoga a part of my daily routine that I truly began to see its effects. I owe my life to yoga. Magic unfolds in my life on a daily basis.

Prior to leaving, a lot of fear-based projection was thrown my way and there were times when I would buy into them. During those times, I would sit in meditation and allow that deep, all-knowing intuitive voice to filter out the fear.

I am so grateful for every lesson, every hardship and every change. Life is a gift and each moment is so fleeting. Embrace it. Love it. Live your life solely for you. I don't mean this in a selfish way but I have found that the only person I can change is myself. I choose to listen to my soul, and live according to its vibration, not someone else's expectation.

Once I found that pure, infinite peace in myself, the change in me had a ripple effect. Somehow all the closest people in my life were affected without there being a discussion. Every second is an opportunity to be more kind, more generous, to learn, to grow, to evolve and to love.

- **Passion:** Being a source of love wherever I am.
- **Purpose:** To raise consciousness and spread a message of truth to all I come into contact with.
- **Vision:** A world that operates from a place of compassion and love.

Jennifer Posner experienced yoga aged 8, but it wasn't until 2005 that she began serious practice. As a publicist and marketing director she has worked with clients like The Wutang Clan, Vivienne Westwood, Urban Decay Cosmetics, and children's charity The Art of Elysium. For five years she has taught yoga to children and their families in the developing world, with the hope of a ripple effect amongst their communities. She draws inspiration from the transformational power of yoga and combines it with her marketing experience through Serenity Flows Yoga. Based in Peru, she is creating global travel guides for yogis.

Website: http://www.serenityflowsyoga.com

Take Action

By Anthony Benenati
Father. Golfer. Surfer. Chef of the House. Gardener. Humanitarian.

Life is about taking action. My story connected with this is simple: actions speak louder than words. It is what one does, not what one says, that makes the difference. We have learned about this by studying the *Gita*. It is all about skilful action.

If you think about it, it is our BELIEFS that get us into trouble with others; it is our beliefs against theirs. A belief system is where stereotypes and biases germinate. It is also the difference between yoga and religion. Religion is about what you BELIEVE. In fact, you have to believe something to be a part of it.

Yoga doesn't care about what you believe ... you don't have to believe in anything ... you just need to practice (take action). And in so doing (with the right teacher) you will learn to take skilful action.

Beliefs can stifle you; stop you dead in your tracks. Think of how many times you are stymied by what you think someone believes about you, or what you think about them.

The Dalai Lama was once asked: 'With so many "gurus" out there, how do you know which one to follow?' He answered: 'You must be like the dog. You must sniff both from the front *and* the back.' Don't get caught up in beliefs; they are like a net that traps everything.

- **Passion:** Live to the fullest, without apology or regret.

- **Purpose:** To teach this to my children.

- **Vision:** My empowered children teaching others to live an empowered life.

Anthony Benenati was introduced to yoga by a girlfriend after an injury. Career-wise he had done just about everything up until that point, from the Air Force to Hollywood film sets. His love of yoga inspired action, and he founded City Yoga in LA in 1999 where the driving philosophy enables work on the body, mind and spirit without judgment, elitism or dogma. (It was sold to YogaWorks in 2013.) Having created a yoga community in the midst of a bustling city centre, and raising money to help *Yoga Gives*, Anthony focus on teaching people how to heal and prevent injury with his playful teaching style.

Do Whatever it Takes

By Hemalayaa
Motivator. Green Thumb. Cook. Doula. Writer.

At heart we are all artists. To stay young at heart, our careers and interests can change many times. Find the belief in yourself to go for your heart's desire, whatever it might be, and just try it. Even if it seems like the wackiest thing, go for it. You will not be satisfied in your life if you don't do the things that you're called to do.

Serve from your highest, most beneficial self. If you could live your life without fear, worry about what others will say, or your own mind saying 'no', what would you do? Go do that right now. Whatever your 'thing' is. Go for it.

Do what it takes. Do what it takes to make your heart smile. Come to a place of joy and live with a smile in your heart. Even if it is the weirdest, funkiest, strangest thing. Go for it.

- **Passion:** Creating joyful experiences through yoga and dance. Bringing laughter and joy out of people.

- **Purpose:** Bridging the child and the adult self together for fabulous fun.

- **Vision:** Bringing a lightness and joy to every person in the world. To conquer the world with laughter.

Hemalayaa's first encounter with yoga was at home with a book, although growing up she had watched her father practice yoga, *pranayama* and meditation. The book was a gift from a friend who, herself not a yogi, thought it might be good for her, and it led to a twelve-week Iyengar course and then a Vedic lifestyle as part of the inner quest to find out what life was all about. With experience in theatre, commercials and TV, Hemalayaa is a natural-born teacher, sharing her yoga-inspired Indian dance through her classes and workshops. Based in Los Angeles, Hemalayaa teaches locally at Exhale and Liberation Yoga Studio, and at international festivals like Bhakti Fest.

Website: http://www.hemalayaa.com

Expand Into Your Edge

By Chris Calarco
Phish-head. Basketball enthusiast. Music geek.

In October 2012 I was at a talk given by philosophy scholar Douglas Brooks in Colorado, where he posed the question: 'What happens when life asks more of you?' I immediately fell in love with the question. So often we are faced with this circumstance: there is too much to do, there are difficult choices to make, and the pressure begins to mount. We are overwhelmed.

It can become clear in these times that life may be asking us to change our usual way of being; to shift our habitual patterns if we want to grow. When fear kicks in we may either want to push through with all our might or shut down completely. However, when life asks more of us, we have a special opportunity consciously to choose who we are and how we want to be. In an uncertain, always changing world, this is our edge.

Our edge is a potent opportunity for growth. If we choose to act with care we can step more fully into our passion, purpose and vision. The edge is ripe because we have to confront confusion and doubt about the 'right' choice to make or the 'best' path to take. Do we quit the job? Start or stop the relationship? Move cities? Say 'I love you'? Time seems to stop. We come face to face with ourselves. We may feel a burning desire to make a choice that feels safe just to maintain the status quo.

This is not so easy to resist when we are inundated with messages like, 'just do it', 'step up', and 'rise to the occasion'. Unfortunately, our cultural values are skewed and our support systems are broken. These sentiments can be valid in the right moment and from the right confidant. However, if we fail to live up to these externally imposed standards their ubiquitous presence has the power to cultivate a harsh inner critic, a gnawing pressure to succeed and lower self-esteem. How can we use these moments to grow in the face of the pressure to succeed?

In his talk, Dr Brooks illuminated a perspective originating in Indian philosophy that aligns with the mainstream work of Dr Brené Brown in her book *The Gifts of Imperfection*. He said in a lecture: 'There is something more *worth it* that is unlike success or failure.'

When life asks more of us we are pushed to the edge of our inner resources and we are called to engage deeply with unconscious habits. Precisely because of this we are invited toward the fertile ground of risk, vulnerability and intimacy. To traverse these scary worlds takes courage. Brooks and Brown both refer us to the Latin root of courage, *cor*, meaning to speak and act with all our heart.

How would an overwhelming edge feel if we could honestly, authentically, and passionately act from the heart? Could we stop the barrelling train toward *success*, and even decrease the terror of impending *failure*? Instead of caring solely about the *results* of our actions could we instead see that the risk of vulnerability is worth more than a quantifiable successful outcome? When we make ourselves vulnerable, people can see our heart. For this reason I believe it is *how* we engage with our edge that is more important.

When we subscribe to the success-failure model, we can easily succumb to the glowing temptation of perfection. We want to win every time, get every promotion, and hit home runs in the most pressure-filled situations. However, when we seek perfection we create impossibly unreasonable expectations for ourselves. We then easily pass these expectations on to others. We begin to add to the pressure; we perpetuate the problem. This fosters anxiety and fuels self-judgement – both of which are rampantly epidemic in the western world. In order to step into our courageous hearts we must be willing to look at what habits are holding us back. If we seek the greatness of whole-hearted effort instead of success we begin to see the human beauty in imperfection.

I urge you to change the paradigm within yourself and out in the world. For far too long we have bludgeoned ourselves with self-abuse. May we recognise that putting our heart on the line will foster more growth than any external idea of success. May we begin to see that patterns of emotional numbing, blame and shirking accountability contract our ability to grow. May we humbly and without shame admit our mistakes, apologise and listen. At the edge of life's challenges may we EXPAND our capabilities and stretch ourselves toward new *inner* terrain. The rest will take care of itself.

- **Passion:** The path of yoga, the power of music.
- **Purpose:** To expand beyond self-imposed limiting boundaries.
- **Vision:** A growing community of people committed to expanding.

Chris Calarco discovered yoga in 2005 at a community centre class. After that he tried out classes at Yoga Union in Portland, Oregon and found a second home. He practised child and family therapy for four years while studying yoga, which he gradually stopped as his commitment to yoga became full time. He's currently working to expand Yoga Union into a Community Wellness Centre while meeting the strict green building requirements of The Living Building Challenge. It is his hope that his yoga is inspirational to his students.

Website: http://chriscalarcoyoga.com

Search For Your Teacher

By Jonathan Monks
Teacher. Explorer. Innovator. Author. Singer.

During the period of our life between the years 20 to 40, we feel jammed full of potential. Our inner fires desire, burn and consume the hours of each day and we passionately search for, and feel-out, ourselves on our surroundings. My advice during this time of great potential and abundant energy is to develop a daily practice where you hone your desired skills.

If it be innovation, then set aside time to create; if it be nourishing the world, then take a practice which nourishes you.

But, most importantly, aim for mastery and to make yourself a living embodiment of your chosen discipline.

To help you do this, find someone who's found what you're looking for and learn from them. Search for your teacher and invest your time in what is taught. Not only will it help you get to where you want to go but also on your journey of discovery you'll nourish the world in the process.

- **Passion:** Discovering what teachers and texts talk of.

- **Purpose:** Is found in the essence of relationship.

- **Vision:** To sing clear and true.

Jonathan Monks began teaching himself yoga in 1989, the same year he took his first Tai Chi class. YogaMonks was born in 2001 to express the relationships he was discovering in his own practice. The method is a blend of traditional *asana* postures and the dynamic movement of Vinyasa, resulting in an original set of core sequences with names like Moon and Ski. He has shared his work at Yoga Games, Nike and British Wheel of Yoga conferences, and published a book, *Pilates Yoga*, in 2002. The studio is in East London and the method finds its way to students in many studios across the city.

Website: http://www.yogamonks.com

Children Are The Real Teachers

By Jo Manuel
Charity Founder. Community Leader. Businesswoman. Mother.
Harmonium Player. Singer. Traveller.

The Dalai Lama says that the world does not need more successful people. He suggests that we need more peacemakers, healers, restorers, storytellers, and lovers. This is what I teach children. There is too much pressure on academic achievement and not enough about learning who we are; how to share our lives with others with honesty and respect; how to be happy and peaceful inside; and how to take care of the beautiful planet that we have the privilege to live on.

At an early age we inherently know what is right and how to do things, but society changes us. We can remind ourselves of these qualities by embodying them ourselves and by doing so set a much needed example for the next generation. Children learn from who we are, not from what we say.

Having said that, children are the real teachers. Those I have had the privilege to share yoga with, many of whom live with special needs, have taught me so much. Through them I have learned the true power of yoga, and the meaning of 'living in yoga'.

I have learned to really love without attachment and to find the depths of unconditional love that resides in me.

I have learned to trust in myself. By trusting the child and surrendering truly, I can live in as much grace as possible.

I have learned that patience comes from that trust. In the space of truly trusting we make a connection to something greater than ourselves. I know that I am fully supported by the Universe, and that sometimes I need to take myself out of the way to allow it.

I have learned the difference between intention and expectation, and the power of pure thought.

I have learned to live in my heart with as much honesty as I can find. In that place I can meet others with openness, honesty, love and compassion.

I have learned to believe in the power of gratitude for everything that comes into my life, and for life itself, even in the most challenging moments. These moments have much to teach me.

Ultimately I have learned to meet everyone as people, beyond the limitations we see on the surface. We ALL have special needs, and we are ALL special.

- **Passion:** The ability of yoga to open our hearts and connect us with each other.
- **Purpose:** To make yoga available to everyone, irrespective of race, creed, religious beliefs, or financial wellbeing.
- **Vision:** For every child to have the opportunity and tools to reach their fullest potential.

Jo Manuel stepped into her first yoga class in 1972, a moment that changed her life. In her twenties and thirties she was in the entertainment business, but it was yoga that allowed her to connect with her tribe. She founded The Special Yoga Centre in London in 2004 which offered yoga therapy and mindfulness as an aid to enhance the child's capacity to learn within mainstream and special needs schools. Although SYC went into administration in 2013, her work with children continues. Jo is propelled by her belief that yoga helps us to love and believe in ourselves, gives us strength and courage, and opens our hearts.

Website: http://specialyoga.org.uk

Start at the End

By Raphan Kebe
Innovator. Body worker. Photographer. Musician.

I sometimes start my self-practice, and even my classes, with the end. Meaning that I will do at the beginning what I'm supposed to end with. Besides showing me the complexity of what I am trying to achieve, it also very much shows me the simplicity of it all.

By understanding the hard and the soft, the 'tough to negotiate', or the 'already acquired' skill set (the parts of what I am trying to accomplish), be it a physical posture or an energetically enhanced kinaesthetic understanding, I am *given* a plan of action. More importantly I am truly gifted with the ability to assess whether I am truly turned on and as such very motivated to apply myself to the task ahead, or simply and honestly not interested in pursuing the means to the 'end' I thought I wanted. So, long story short, following your passion is to me being able equally to enjoy and put up with, let's be honest here, the amount of work required to reach your goal.

By putting yourself ahead in time (and there are many ways to do that), I believe you will eventually be able to assess what is required of you. Then comes the beginning of the end, crunch time, decision time and game time: are you going to victimise yourself or are you going to empower yourself? The choice is actually yours. If it is your passion, your purpose, your vision, then it will have to be your work that turns an 'end to a means' into a 'means to an end'. This, I also believe, is what yoga is all about. So grow with and within, my friend: it is all there in the beginning, so you decide if you keep at it in the end.

- **Passion:** Movement.
- **Purpose:** To guide practitioners towards a freer expression of their own yoga path.
- **Vision:** To be engaged, yet relaxed, on my path.

Raphan Kebe's path to yoga was unexpected. Originally a photographer, Raphan moved to London to study music. Suffering back and wrist pain during his studies led to training in massage therapy and structural bodywork. Pilates led to his first Hatha Yoga class, which led to yoga teacher-training in Canada. Raphan has since gone on to develop Yoga in

Motion, a dynamic teacher-training programme, and continues to evolve Space and Flow Yoga, a style that combines the Feldenkrais method, the Yogamonks yoga style, and Zen Buddhism, as well as Capoeira and Contemporary Dance. He teaches yoga across London, and hosts retreats in Turkey and France.

Website: http://raphan.co.uk/

Find Your Spirit and Always Refer Back to It

By Gemma Ford
Entrepreneur. Wife. Life Coach. Lifestyle Designer.

For me the spirit in your life is that connection to the divine: God, nature, your true self, light, love – any or all of the above. At different times that connection to spirit comes through different channels. For example, when I am swimming in the sea at sunset the beauty of nature is filling me up. During my meditation in the few moments when my mind is completely quiet, the connection is the utmost peace and certainty I find inside me.

I have had times, and still have times, when everything seems so uncertain. My path is in question and I wonder how I got here? At these times the question of where I am going seems so huge and unanswerable, and all I can do is keep that connection alive, get more creative about ways to find spirit in my life, and have faith that clarity will come. What we do changes, and what we think is changeable, but our true nature (our connection to something higher) remains consistent, no matter what the situation. It makes us equal; it grounds us; it sets us free and makes it all worth it. Find the spirit in your life and always refer back to it.

- **Passion:** Helping people feel better and better, and eventually wonderful.

- **Purpose:** To pass on the awesome and life-enhancing lessons, practices and philosophies of yoga to as many people as I can.

- **Vision:** To make yoga available and affordable to people all over the world.

Gemma Ford tried yoga while at school when relaxation techniques helped her sleep during exam time. She was an affiliate marketing manager in London's new media industry for three years before traveling to India in 2009 to explore her interest in yoga and Eastern philosophies. Returning to the UK with a desire to set out on a new life path, she moved to the surfing town of Cornwall on the south coast of England where she launched Love Yoga Online in January 2012. Now re-sculpting her own business vision, she is supporting her dad's entrepreneurial vision and training as a life coach.

Life Moves Pretty Quick

By Aimee Hartley
Rollerblader. Outdoor Swimmer. Surfer. Practising Poet. Dancer.

Dance on rising
Sing before you sleep
Follow your gut instincts
Love before you leap.

Search for something
You want others to find
Love your body
And master your mind.

Love like Paris, eat like Rome
Decorate your heart with a colourful shade
Read more, spend less, travel alone
Always find the bright side of a badly made day.

Embrace everyone you meet like your dearest friend
Ask strangers for words on life and art
Love life's wrinkles, its skin smiling back at you
Travel to places that move the centre of your heart.

Smile like you mean it
Sweat four times a week
Learn how to breathe well
Practice what you seek.

Say thank you every day to the people you love
Listen to children and watch how you grow
Take ... your ... time. Live hours well
Inhale deeply and learn to touch your toes.

Practice relaxing, embrace change
Turn fear into excitement, transform hate into love
Gamble with a twist, don't you dare stick.

Love
Love, laugh and
Love.
Because life moves pretty quick.

- **Passion:** Helping people reach their full potential in life.

- **Purpose:** I find my life's purpose is continuously transforming. For now I believe my purpose in life is to teach children and adults to understand the importance of breathing well.

- **Vision:** My vision for the future is to teach children and adults to improve their breathing. Ideally I would like to take the Transformational Breathing technique into schools in the UK and beyond.

Aimee Hartley's mum introduced her to yoga when she was aged 24. She was inspired by her seventy-five-year old teacher who demonstrated grace, flexibility and humour, and she vowed to become a yoga teacher herself. She's had a varied career from PR to jewellery design, and launched PR Fit in

2008, a PR consultancy specialising in health and wellbeing. She opened The Breathing Room based in London's Liverpool Street in 2011. As well as running her own transformational breathing retreats, she continues to organise yoga retreats on behalf of fellow yogis in the UK and Bali. But most exciting is her newest role yet: mum.

Website: http://thebreathingroom.co.uk

Blaze On With Fearless Love

By Leza Lowitz
Writer. Poet. Translator. Mother. Traveller.

If you have a dream, it's because your soul is yearning to manifest it. No one else has your own unique brand of talent, passion, experience and vision. Don't be afraid to follow your dreams, no matter how wild, and embrace your shadow. That thing that won't stop calling to you? That's the path you need to take. Blaze on with fearless love.

Listen to your inner voice

I'm in a place called Haiku, Hawaii, on retreat. On the second morning I sit down to meditate on the *lanai*, breathing in the wet, fresh air. The island spirits call to me through the hot, damp mists. After what might be three hours or three minutes, a voice calls out in my head. It is very clear, and strong. I do not open my eyes.

'You must go to Tokyo and open up a yoga studio,' it says.

I sit and breathe deeply. As if I hadn't heard it, the message is repeated. I wait for more messages. It could be ten minutes or an hour, but none come. When the meditation feels finished, I open my eyes.

Who spoke to me? Was it my own inner guidance? Was it the island's goddess, Pele? Her energy radiates from the powerful volcano nearby. From a book at the retreat centre's library, I learn that Pele is the quintessential power woman – sometimes young and beautiful, other times an old crone. She has the power to destroy, the power to create. She's a wanderer, expelled from her homeland. Finally, she settles on the largest mountain in the world, Mauna Loa. To this day her sacred fires burn there, high above the sea. Is this why she wants me to leave my home in California and return to Japan, deep into the ring of fire? Do I really want to go from one fault-line to another, just when I'm feeling settled and at home?

Follow the Path

I turn these thoughts around in my mind, entertaining the possibilities. I have no intention of going back to Tokyo, where I'd lived in my twenties, or of opening a yoga studio, much less starting a business in a foreign country. I'm happy in California, happy in my quiet little life, teaching yoga at a small studio, writing and helping my husband with translation work. I dismiss the message. It's just too crazy to consider.

Two years go by. Then my husband goes to Tokyo to visit his father, and comes back to the States having made the decision to return to Japan. *Will you come?* he asks.

America is at war. The economy is not favourable to freelance translators right now, when outsourcing is cheap. And my husband is *chonan*.

In Japan, *chonan* is a serious business. *Chonan* means the first-born son and heir to the family name and fortunes. It also means that the family is ultimately his responsibility, and that of the *yome*, the lady of the house. Which, now that his mother has passed away, would be me.

I sit down to meditate on my future. Our future. I don't really want to go back to Tokyo, the busy life, the pollution and the stress. But I love my husband, and want to be with him. And I know that a good marriage is partly based on compromise, even sacrifice. The root of the word sacrifice is *sacred*. In the highest sense, sacrifice is to do something completely for someone else with no personal gain. As an independent American woman that idea takes some getting used to.

But what would I do in Tokyo? I'd lived there for four years during my twenties in the economy's 'Bubble Years', when I wrote for newspapers and magazines, taught English, and worked as a copywriter for a cosmetics company. It was a fun life, a fast life, and a life that was great then. But California had made 'mush' of me, and I love my slow pace, my friends and my yoga. 'My' yoga.

I remember the message I got in *haiku* about opening up a yoga studio in Tokyo.

'Do you think I can do that?' I ask Shogo.

'Anything's possible,' he says.

'I'll take that as a yes,' I reply.

I Google 'yoga studios in Tokyo'. Only two come up. The yoga boom hasn't happened yet. Maybe it's a good time to go. Some people tell me it's ridiculous to bring 'western yoga' to the land of Zen. I don't listen. I have finally learned to listen to the voice within.

Blaze On With Fearless Love

Starting a business in a foreign country is daunting, but I try not to think about all the things I can't do. I feel guided to move forward. I keep moving, one step at a time. Besides which, I've ordered thirty yoga bolsters, fifty blankets, and twenty-five-pound sandbags from a supplier in San Francisco. I've also ordered thirty silk neck pillows and lavender-filled eye bags. Why? Having lived in busy Tokyo before, I want to practice and teach restorative yoga, a deeply relaxing prac- tice anyone can do. You just surrender to the props and let them hold you. It's like lying back in the arms of mother earth, swaddled in love.

The props will be coming soon, and I don't have anywhere to put them. I need to rent a place, and now! We find a place in central Tokyo, close to the main train line. It's funky, but it opens up to empty space and light. In California, we'd been living surrounded by the sea and the mountains, and open space and green. In Tokyo, there's really not much green out- side of a cup of tea. I want to make the studio green and calm and feminine. I want to create a little oasis where people can discover and be their authentic selves through yoga and meditation.

An architect friend takes some bamboo from our garden and makes a round moon-window shape. I call the studio Sun and Moon Yoga, after the yin and yang of life and the union of the side channels into our central channel, where goodness and contentment abides. When the remodel is done, I'm ready to open. But the props are held up in customs. They have to check every bolster, sandbag and eye pillow for drugs. Finally we get the green light and open our doors.

At first only a handful of students come. I try not to panic (remember to trust that voice inside). After all, it was in *haiku* that I'd heard it. Japan is the birthplace of *haiku*. The gods have to be happy, right? While waiting for everyone to come, I come to a realisation that I myself have not yet arrived. So I sit down in my little studio in Tokyo, being grateful for all that has taken me to this moment.

Light streams in through the windows. I try to stay in the light, keep practising and trusting, letting myself embody the space with my own practice, my breath. Then students come. They do partner yoga with people they've never spo- ken to, touch people they've never seen before. They laugh and they cry. Teachers show up. We offer community classes, even though people tell me it will never fly in Japan, where brands and luxury goods signify value. It flies.

In a city of millions of people, we do something revolution-ary. We make friends with strangers. We make friends with ourselves. We make a kind of peace in a city of chaos. We find silence in a world full of noise. Before we know it, we have a *sangha* – a community. On our first anniversary we have a party. After everyone has gone home, I lie back on the bol-sters, letting myself be enveloped in the sun and the moon. I feel grateful and humbled. I hear another voice. It says: 'Blaze on with fearless love.'

- **Passion:** Speaking and living your truth.

- **Purpose:** To teach. To love.

- **Vision:** Life as poetry. Poetry as life.

Leza Lowitz discovered yoga in 1994 and considers it the best year of her life (since she claims to have been a certified mess beforehand). She opened Sun & Moon Yoga in Japan, and has enjoyed the challenge of doing that in a foreign country. Also a talented writer, she co-authors books on subjects like Jap-anese and Sanskrit. She writes young adult fiction about a kick-ass female ninja like *Jet Black and the Ninja Wind*, and has combined her passion for yoga and poetry through *Yoga Poems: Lines to Unfold By*. She loves the magical alchemy of yoga, and feels blessed to share its empowering quality with others.

Website: http://sunandmoon.jp

Absolutely on Purpose

Chapter 6: The Workbooks

The Workbooks are spaces to explore who you are, right here, right now. With that clarity you can approach your passion, purpose and vision from a fresh angle. Each one is designed to bring to life the juicy, visionary, common sense nuggets you've just read in Chapter 5.

If you're following the 'fast' or 'medium' reading strategy, rest assured you can dive straight in.

The Workbooks are designed to kick-start two things:

1. A **Clean Slate** – so that you can *start empty*.
2. A **Passion, Purpose, and Vision Brainstorm** (PPV) – to brainstorm your PPV and play with their expression.

These spaces capture time for you to reflect the subtle aspects and forces at play in your life – the ones that determine your experience, perspective and choices without you even realising. Once the slate is clean it becomes a space to create and express your own PPV. How? It's easier to create a vision of the future if you can acknowledge the present with a little more clarity. My intention is for both these things to affect a shift in perspective, a fresh approach, and a way to *start empty* before colouring in the detail.

Use the Blank Space

I created blank space in the workbooks to give the impression of 'mental space'. Even if you don't have paper with you, you can use the blank space to prompt your thinking. The blank space is indicated by a line: ....

Confront Your Resistance

Be aware: it might be that not all ideas presented resonate with you. I've tried to present a good mix of logical and esoteric ideologies. How you interpret and combine them with your own knowledge and experience determines the wisdom you invoke. Your agreement is not necessary for them to be valuable; in fact disagreement will encourage clarity as your own ideas begin to crystallise. This is how your own wisdom manifests.

Dig Deeper

I urge you one thing: if concepts seem far-fetched or bizarre, spend some time with them first before moving on, perhaps even longer than on other sections. Who knows what breakthroughs you'll have by confronting the things that press your buttons? Simply by entertaining new ideas you start to see through a different lens, and what you begin to see and feel might be quite different too. These are the most useful nuggets. Ultimately I recommend that you employ a pic'n'pix strategy – and remember: this is not a formula but a voyage of discovery.

Clean Your Slate More Than Once

Cleaning the slate is a process similar to peeling an onion. *Clean Your Slate* once, and you're exploring the first layer. If you come back to it again you'll uncover some deeper truths. Again, and you go still deeper. Your slate gets cleaner and cleaner the more layers you peel away. I encourage you to take a break between each round, then see what you find in the next one.

Get ready to read, write, and unfurl your brilliance.

Chapter 7: Clean Your Slate

'Clean Your Slate' is designed to aid your reflection on the subtle aspects and forces at play in your life. The questions require your full dedication and focus because they don't have any magic powers in themselves. The quality of your thinking and feeling as you reflect on the questions, and the degree of truth and contemplation with which you answer them, will determine their usefulness in helping you to 'Clean Your Slate'.

Whether these forces are subtle or overt, the themes covered in this section affect what we do, how we do it, and why we do it. There are no correct answers, only truthful ones, so you needn't worry about passing or failing. The only conclusion is the awareness you derive from your answers. As you come face to face with your most raw, unapologetic self, I hope that this inspires clarity and empowers you to follow your passion, purpose and vision.

Remember that it's what you do with the awareness you encounter that will determine your transformation. I loathe self-help books that prescribe a formula for transformation, as though if you follow a formula everything will magically transform. It doesn't and it won't, because you are as unique as the person who wrote it. What inspired their transformation will not necessarily empower your own. We create our own meaning as we collect inspiration from others and apply it in a way that works for us, and that's when it becomes transformative. If any one thing worked for everyone, there wouldn't be so many books. There is no magic bullet. You are fully accountable for transforming knowledge into wisdom; that responsibility is yours alone.

I've drawn out insights that tell me a story from beginning to end. It's how I make sense of the collection, bring it to life, and extract meaning that resonates with me. I've shared my insights and ideas with you to bring them to life and asked you questions to bring you deeper into the story with me.

Each contribution in 'Chapter 5: Visionary Common Sense' will resonate with you differently; in fact they might speak to you differently each time you read them. Some you might love, some might irritate the crap out of you, some might make no sense at all. Even so, you've created your own meaning from the collection, and maybe even highlighted and written down the lines you love the most. Like I have, you will have created your own story and developed your own wisdom. This I love. I hope you do, too.

How to Use This Section

- **Over five weeks:** Complete one chapter each week.

- **Over a weekend:** Select one chapter for a mini 'Clean Your Slate' intensive.

- **Over an evening:** Scan the chapter summaries to cherry-pick the exercises and troubleshoot key aspects immediately.

What You'll Need

A pen and lots of paper.

How to Approach the Questions

1. Take a deep breath and feel into each question. Give it a few moments to sit with you, and see what comes to you from that space. Try not to dwell on anything for too

long; usually the first words you *hear* are your inner voice speaking.

2. If you get stuck, go away and do something else. Let the questions percolate. When you come back, your truth may have crystallised without you having done any hard work at all.

Contributor quotes inspired the backbone of this workbook, but you'll find pop culture quotes, too. We may categorise yoga as a physical practice, but its philosophy has found its way into mainstream culture; its wisdom is around us all the time.

Are you ready to clean your slate?

Absolutely on Purpose

Chapter 8: Listen, Feel, Allow

Chapter Snapshot

- Find Your Flow (and Go With It)
- Inhabit the Moment
- Step Out of Your Comfort Zone
- What Are You Thinking?
- What Are You Doing?
- What Does Your Heart Say?
- What Is Your Body Telling You?

Find Your Flow (and Go With It)

Control is an illusion of the mind to try and keep me safe. Instead it is keeps me prisoner. The trick is to let go of the control and discover freedom.

– Laura Knowles

You don't have to be a carefree hippy to go with the flow. Going with the flow, combined with a crystal-clear vision, is a clean pathway to living *Absolutely on Purpose*. But it can be hard to go with the flow when we are planned up to our eyeballs.

Planning is an essential skill. It gives us the confidence to navigate from A to B. But it can also hold us back if the plans are too rigid, and if there are too many! We plan to make things more simple – to organise our day, meet all our commitments and to manifest the 'five year plan'. But if we're not careful, life can become a never ending to-do list devoid of flow, spontaneity and new opportunities.

If you find that your time is characterised by to-do lists and schedules, you're not 'in flow'. When we allow for a degree of flexibility in our plans, we open our world to spontaneity and opportunity. We open ourselves up to inspiration and creativity. We improve our ability to 'listen', 'feel' and 'allow'. If you've ever said: 'I can't do this because I've got to do this,' think about how to make it a more 'active' choice: 'If I do *this* now, how can I jiggle things around so I can do *that* later on?'

When we're 'in flow' we become more 'active' in the direction of our lives, and able to make decisions based on the present rather than on the past or the future. When you invite a vivid vision and a flexible attitude to coexist in a 'state of flow', you're at the top of your game.

Truth is One. Paths are many.

– Alex Grant

I'm a strategist and a natural planner, but I'm also a self-confessed flow artist. My path twists and turns as I flow with opportunities presented on the way. My trajectory might change, but that does not mean the vision does. It might manifest in a different way, shape, or form, but it is guaranteed to manifest bigger, better, stronger if I've followed the clearest, brightest path along the way. I believe that I can only ever live in the present, not some moment in the near or distant future, so I make decisions based on the feelings and information I have at hand. These might come from conversations, experiences, or gut instinct. They might involve leaving a job, a relationship, or moving country. I've been labelled mad, careless and irresponsible. Yet these decisions are in line with *my* truth, *my* dreams, and *my* goals. I trust that the decisions I make are right for me. They've guided me to knock-your-socks-off places, people, adventures, and successes. Writing a book wasn't even part of my vision five years ago, but manifested as a result of opportunities and experiences that happened along the way. (If you told me then that I'd be publishing a book in 2013, I would have considered you certifiable!)

Opportunities present themselves spontaneously, tantalising in all their splendour, only to disappear moments later. Going with the flow means that you can ascertain – within moments – whether these opportunities can propel you forward, whether they will hold you back, or whether they could radically and positively alter your trajectory forever.

If you are in touch with your truth you can accept or reject opportunities in an instant, as an act of co-creation. You take on a creative and collaborative role in the design of your own life. If you gloss over opportunities because they don't align with your six-month/one-year/five-year plan, you might be missing an opportunity either to supersize your vision or sculpt a completely new one.

We reach into our highest potential when our vision aligns with our passions and purpose. Listening, feeling and allowing helps you tap into your truth in each moment, a strategy that eventually becomes your *modus operandi*. Hotwired to your truth, you become a consummate flow artist.

Raghunath's ladder metaphor is an excellent one: you can use your truth in any matter to determine whether you're climbing the right ladder against the right wall. Don't get me wrong, dedication and focus are noble traits, but if you're working towards a vision that does not align with your passion and purpose, the climb will be arduous and your dedication and focus will become the very things that shield you from opportunities to switch ladders and pitch against a different wall. Going with your flow means you can assess, consistently, whether your climb is congruent with your vision (and worthy of your dedication and focus).

Going with the flow is responding to cues from the universe. When you go with the flow, you're surfing Life force. It's about wakeful trust and total collaboration with what's showing up for you.

– Danielle LaPorte

Are you a flow artist? Circle your answer.

YES / NO

Do you have a plan / vision / goal? Circle your answer.

YES / NO

How far ahead have you planned? Circle your answer.

6 months / 1 year / 5 years / other: ....

My 6-month / 1-year / 5-year / other plan is: ....

....

....

....

....

....

How flexible is your plan? (10=flexi like a yogi, 1=rigid like steel) ....

What opportunities have you turned down (because they didn't align with your plan)**?**

1. ....

2. ....

3. ....

4. ....

5. ....

6. ....

7. ....

8. ....

9. ....

10. ....

Inhabit the Moment

Be present to the experience of the moment.

– Adriana Cortazzo

To become a flow artist and make trajectory-altering decisions in real time, we need to master the art of inhabiting each moment. But wait a minute. How do you maintain a vivid vision, follow your plan, AND inhabit the moment, all at the same time?

If you think of your vision as the shining light at the end of the tunnel, and your plans as the path towards it, then this very moment right here, right now is the entrance. They co-exist beautifully because they are part of the same path (beginning, middle, and end). Your ability to inhabit the moment makes everything else possible. It requires discipline and regular practice, and is an art form in itself, but we can all be experts in it. It's a delicate blend of love, appreciation, and awareness of what you're doing right now (whatever it is).

I used to be a time-traveller. I spent hours at my desk astral projecting myself into the future, looking forward to exotic travels and simply surviving Monday through Friday. I was only semi-present (living a half-life) to the potential pleasure of the moment because I was avoiding confrontation with the question: 'What am I doing?' While effectively avoiding the pain of the moment, I was unaware that 'the moment' is the space in which we propel ourselves towards our vision. I could kick myself for missing the opportunity to find magic in the mundane – by simply showing up and inhabiting each second.

Whatever you're doing – no matter how mundane, boring, or frustrating – by giving any task 120 per cent of your attention, and focusing on the quality, the process, or your sensory experience, you can benefit from inhabiting the moment.

The more awake and present you are the more you will find joy and contentment in the everyday and mundane.

– Mark Davies

Do you see the start of your working week as an opportunity to co-create a new experience? Are you guilty of astral projection? Cut it out. It's great to dream, to hold a vision for your future, but not at the expense of the here and now. (We'll look at how to reverse-engineer your vision back to the present moment later, in the section called 'Start at the End' in Chapter 12.)

We are most mindful – or in the moment – when we're doing something we really love. Time seems to stand still as
we hover in suspended animation, enjoying the experience,
feeling, touch, taste, smell, sound or sight of something that
makes us feel 'alive'.

What are you doing when you become lost in the moment?
When you forget what you're doing? I lose myself in Spanish cinema, juicy mangoes from Pakistan, and barefoot walks
along empty, white, sandy beaches. Get specific.

1. ....

2. ....

3. ....

4. ....

5. ....

6. ....

7. ....

8. ....

9. ....

10. ....

How much time do you spend doing these things each week?
Add them up and see what your 'inhabit the moment' score is.

I inhabit the moment .... hrs / mins each week.

Which of these things can you do more often? How else can
you add more magic to your day?

Tips for inhabiting the moment

- **Play with children.** Have you ever noticed how children play? They are the ultimate flow artists, riding the wave of time like world-class surfers. They co-create with the universe through imagination and play. Borrow someone's kids (if you don't have your own) and play!

- **Spend time with animals.** There's nothing like a good game of fetch. Volunteer to walk a dog at a local shelter, or for someone who is elderly or housebound. Joy, love and licks. Lush.

- **Watch animals in the wild.** Witness a herd of elephant bulls arrive at a watering hole ten minutes apart from each other. Plod. Plod. Plod. All your senses alert; each sound vibrating through every cell in your body. Watching animals in their natural habitat is mesmerising. It stops astral projection dead in its tracks.

More tips (if you can't leave the house)

- **Wiggle your toes.** If you can't get outside, or are at work or somewhere busy, just wiggle your toes. You can return from anywhere by moving your body. Try it now. WIGGLE THEM!

- **Write a *haiku*.** Unleash your wild creative force (yes, you DO have one!) and write a poem. I am addicted to *haiku*, a Japanese poem of seventeen *on* (phonetic sounds in Japanese poetry rather than syllables as commonly thought), five on the first line, seven on the second, and five on the third. *Haiku* are addictive. They're fun and easy – just make up any old gibberish and feel the poet start to flow out of you. Your turn. Create three right now, and send one to me at haiku@absolutelyonpurpose.com. Here's one of mine:

Chapter 8: Listen, Feel, Allow

Chocolate cupcakes

Flavouring my lips and tongue –

Icing on my nose

- **Play a game.** Games are as good as poetry. Sudoko, solitaire, crosswords ... go nuts! Fire up your competitive spirit. Dice and cards are my weakness. Give me a game of Yahtzee or Rummy and watch me inhabit the moment!

- **Clean.** Find something really dirty and scrub it till it's clean. Get your grandma to bring over her silverware for a good polish (just don't get too high on the fumes). Housework is very absorbing. Make your bathroom sink or bedroom windows sparkle.

- **Cook.** I love to cook. From scratch. When you make time to prepare brownies and sit on the counter to lick the cookie dough off a wooden spoon, lovingly pat sea salt and olive oil on the inside of a whole giant sea bass before stuffing it with fennel and lemon and baking it, or prepare guacamole by squishing the avocados and other ingredients through your fingers, you are completely present. And well fed. Try making chocolate cupcakes.

- **Eat.** Slowly eat a piece of chocolate. Meditate on the taste, texture, or smell. In the film *City of Angels*, Maggie (Meg Ryan) describes the taste of a pear as soft sandpaper on her tongue. Be inventive. Use your in-built thesaurus. Think of ways to express your experience (or to hell with that and just enjoy it).

- **Get lost.** If getting lost in the moment is what we're talking about here, why not actually GET LOST? Go on a hike you've never done before or drive to a place you've never seen before. Go to a new city, ditch your lonely planet app and mobile phone, and immerse yourself in a full sensory experience. Chat to locals to find your way, discover quaint cafés when you take a wrong turn, and get caught in a downpour without your umbrella. Take out the convenience. Put the adventure back in. It's harder than ever to get lost. But sometimes it's the only way you can find the present again.

Step Out of Your Comfort Zone

When you are bored, tired, indifferent, or practising avoidance, those are cues that you are sleeping and your eyes, brain and heart need opening.

–Ted Grand

One of the greatest challenges to the art of flow is the comfort zone. Normal life. Sleep state or semi-consciousness. Hamster on a wheel. Routine. Whatever you call it, it's dead weight. We spend years compiling a compendium of normal. We know what we like. We know what we love. We know how everything works. But we are semi-asleep to our full potential if we don't step outside of this state. Challenge is the birthplace of personal transformation. Excitement and enthusiasm for new experiences awakens our consciousness to a new way of being. And did you know that the root meaning of enthusiasm is *divine inspiration*? Doing something new or differently is the best way to inject that into your life.

Stepping out of your comfort zone is not just important – it's essential. If you don't challenge your boundaries, your comfort zone will shrink, and it will keep shrinking until all that is left is a tiny box, a prison of your own making – physically, mentally, spiritually and emotionally. If you never step outside of your box, it will never grow. And neither will your experience. (Or you.)

Travel takes me out of my comfort zone. It anchors me in excitement and enthusiasm for life. It's a lens through which to experience people, places, food and culture. For me it creates a sense of expansion, growth and propulsion. I've turned every decision into an opportunity to travel: study, jobs, projects and the pursuit of a location independent lifestyle. Everything revolves around the excitement and enthusiasm that travel creates. For a very long time it was the only way I knew how to step off the wheel, but it's not the only way to do it. What do you love doing that can inspire your own expansion? How can you use this to regularly step out of your comfort zone and lean into your edge (maybe even fall off it)?

I want to know if your happiness is your pursuit in life and if every minute of your existence you are awake to your consciousness and filled with excitement for that experience.

– Adriana Cortazzo

What would happen if you stepped out of your zone? If you broke from routine? If you spoke to a stranger at the bus stop every day? If you did one thing each week that terrified you? If you started freelancing? If you took up piano/ guitar/ trombone lessons? If you learnt a new language? If you quit your job to go travelling? If you put your spare room on airb-nb.com? If you wrote a business plan for that crazy recurring idea you have? If you signed up for an online creative writing course? If you showed up for aerial trapeze lessons? If you slept in a hammock instead of your bed? If you danced in your living room naked (curtains open or closed is up to you!)? If you moved house / neighbourhood / city / country?

What is your comfort zone? How would you describe it? We all have one. Some of us are more practiced at living outside of it, but we all have one. To start with, think about your routines in the areas of food, work/career and relationships. Your average week. What feels safe, normal, *comfortable*? You might find it helpful to describe your average day or week (average by definition means usual or ordinary).

My average day:

....

....

....

....

....

My average week:

....

....

....

....

....

....

....

....

....

What could you do to shake up your world? Could you:

- Eat raw food for a whole week?
- Date someone outside of your 'type'?
- Go to a movie or out to dinner by yourself?
- Join a dragon boat-racing club?
- Talk to four strangers every week? (When people tell me NOT to talk to strangers, I often reply: 'Only the ones that give me candy'. Because, seriously, I've learnt so much from conversations that last mere minutes.)

These might be things you've thought of before but didn't have the *cojones* to do ...

1. ....

2. ....

3. ....

4. ....

5. ....

6. ....

7. ....

8. ....

9. ....

10. ....

What are some of the bigger things you could do to step outside of your comfort zone? You don't *have* to do anything as dramatic as quit your job, leave a relationship (unless that would emancipate you from a spiralling vortex) or go travelling, but you *could*! Sell your house and buy a boat...? This list might include the more bizarre or wacky things you've thought of doing.

1. ....

2. ....

3. ....

4. ....

5. ....

6. ....

7. ....

8. ....

9. ....

10. ....

What Are You Thinking?

We always have what we wish for in life. Often we just don't know our subconscious mind enough to know what it is projecting; we are the fruit of our thoughts.

– Lawrence Quirk

Our thoughts play a crucial role in the design of our day, week, year, vision and ultimately our lives. Our thinking affects us on a physical, mental, emotional and spiritual level. When something makes us sad we cry. When something makes us feel nervous we get butterflies. When an idea inspires us, we feel 'alive'.

Your thought-reaction to an idea or experience determines its effect on you. Become aware of your thoughts and how they affect you.

When I was developing the proposal for this book project, it was vital for my thoughts to support my desire to create it. I was acutely aware that the people I come in contact with and the media I consume every day impact the quality of my thoughts. I designed my workday to make sure I spent time with colleagues who inspired me and had quality 'chat'. I devoted my social time to smart, supportive friends who make me laugh. I immersed myself in the literature, podcasts and blogs of the authors, entrepreneurs and motivational speakers whom I admire the most. I also got up an hour earlier so that I could work in a café where the baristas are friendly and laugh a lot. I created a real and virtual network that short-circuited negative thinking. Not 100 per cent, but enough to let me get on with it.

Is it possible for you to spend more time with the people and media that improve the quality of your thinking? Are you prepared to highlight things and delete those that affect its quality? If your mind is filled with quality thoughts, the voices of fear and doubt are harder to hear (and the more muffled they are the better).

For there is nothing either good or bad, but thinking makes it so. To me it is a prison.

– Hamlet, Shakespeare, Hamlet (Act 2, Scene 2)

Our thoughts are affected by the people and media we come into contact with every day.

Make a list of the most positive and inspiring people in your social circle. They make you laugh so hard you pee your pants. They transform your utter disasters into life-altering perspectives. Just seeing them makes you forget the shitty day you've had. Their smiles heal all wounds.

1. ....

2. ....

3. ....

4. ....

5. ....

6. ....

7. ....

8. ....

9. ....

10. ....

Can you spend more time with them?

Make a list of the most positive and inspiring people in your place of work or business. They are the people with solutions, and answers to questions. Their footprints inspire your career path. They are open-door people. Go for coffee with them. Ask them questions. They might agree to mentor you on a formal or an informal level. Communicate with them as an equal and, if they are worthy of inspiring you, they will joyously oblige.

1. ....

2. ....

3. ....

4. ....

5. ....

Make a list of public figures that inspire you. These could be authors, entrepreneurs, businesses or motivational speakers. You can spend more time with them through their literature, blogs and podcasts. Bookmark them, subscribe to them, follow them. For those who spend much of their time working solo, this is essential. Having mentors and being part of a tribe is inspiring and uplifting.

1. ....

2. ....

3. ....

4. ....

5. ....

*Consumption of mass media takes away our **power** ... and leaves us feeling empty and helpless, convincing us that we can't change the world.*

– Charley Patton

Audit your social media. Un-follow those with pointless, meaningless, irrelevant or negative updates. Make a list of the media you consume throughout the day. Become aware of the quality of the thinking they inspire.

1. ....

2. ....

3. ....

4. ....

5. ....

6. ....

7. ....

8. ....

9. ....

10. ....

Highlight and delete the ones that dull the quality of your thoughts.

Can you add media sources that will inspire and uplift you? Here are five sources that inspire perspective shifts for me:

1. http://www.ted.com

2. http://bigthink.com

3. http://99u.com

4. http://zenhabits.net

5. http://blogcastfm.com

Spend time with media sources that give wings to your passions. Say 'No!' to doom, gloom, glitz and paparazzi.

What Are You Doing?

*If we are not **proactive** in our own lives we might find ourselves falling into all kinds of things we don't actually want to be doing with our time; a job we dislike, an ambition unrealised, eventually depression.*

– Katie Manitsas

We have a lot of time. Say, for example, that you live until you're eighty. That's approximately 701,265 hours. Based on this life expectancy:

• If you're 20, you have 525,949 hours ahead of you.

• If you're 30, you have 438,291 hours ahead of you.

• If you're 40, you have 350,632 hours ahead of you.

• And so on.

But shit happens. We are often reminded how precious life is, and how high the stakes are. Illness and tragedy strike without warning, reframing our perspective a second too late. Life can be fleeting. Yet each twenty-four hour period holds an opportunity for the perfect experience to unfold, provided we spend our precious time wisely. Can you spend more of yours doing the things you love?

Things we love to do = creative

Things we don't like to do = counter-creative

Time, like money, is currency. If we're not proactive about how we spend it, we'll never have enough. If we're not mindful of our spend it might be allocated to 'counter-creative' activities that take us further away from our passion, purpose and vision.

Counter-creative activities are things we do out of obligation, procrastination, distraction and habit. If we use our time for these activities, what we love to do gets sidelined because we 'lack' time. The closest we come to doing the things we love is thinking and talking about them. Worse still, we feel unsatisfied and unfulfilled, and seek instant gratification to fill the void. Quick-fix pleasures compensate us, but we enjoy them at the expense of deep fulfilment. So we travel further down the rabbit hole.

This feeling of 'something is missing' is both the fuel for our practice (it drives us to be seekers) and our biggest hindrance (because most of us get confused about the best way to fill that void).

— Katie Manitsas

My ultimate counter-creative act was astral projection. I spent hours at my desk, wondering if there was something better I could be doing with my time and dreaming of future travels. Perhaps enough time to study for an online MBA. While waiting for friends to show up, I used to scan social media feeds to kill time. I realised that time was too precious to 'kill', so now I never leave the house without a notebook and pen to write *haiku* and my kindle to read. Sometimes I just wait with my eyes closed. Inhale. Exhale. Identify wasted time so you can find ways to salvage it.

As a marketing strategist I've had a love-hate relationship with social media. In truth, social media platforms have democratised the media landscape and empowered meaningful conversations. They create opportunities for us to listen and be heard; engage and observe; connect with others and find our tribes; be part of a meaningful dialogue and have our say; discover and display; share and comment; and be as accountable and transparent to whatever degree we choose. We can connect, contribute to, and collaborate with our tribes globally in real time. But at what cost?

Are you more responsive to your alerts and messages than the person you are actually with? Do you fill a spacious moment with a cursory glance at a social feed instead of using it as an opportunity for self-reflection? Is your attention permanently fragmented by bite-size data compromising deep thought? Are you addicted to superficial information at the expense of genuine wisdom?

In the *Bhagavad Gita*, (a 700-verse Hindu scripture about the adventures of Arjuna and his guide Lord Krishna) actions are characterised as either done in ignorance, in passion, or in goodness.

What is the nature of your social media behaviour? Is it creative or counter-creative?

_____

Time is what we want most, but what we use worst.

– William Penn, English property entrepreneur and philosopher

When we do things that we don't really want to do, or can't do, it drains us of our energy and vitality, uses up precious time, and distracts us from our true calling.

Make a list of everything you did today. Against each activity, mark down whether it's creative or counter-creative:

Creative – supports your passion, purpose and vision. These activities energise you.

Counter-creative – characterised by obligation, procrastination, distraction and habit. These activities drain you.

How many hours were creative and energising?

....

How many hours were counter-creative and draining?

....

In general, what do you dislike doing? Think of the things you do out of obligation, procrastination, distraction or habit. (Job, social media, eating, social functions, overtime.) How much time do you spend doing each every week?

1. ....

2. ....

3. ....

4. ....

5. ....

Add the total time spent doing these activities each week:

.... [hours] .... [mins]

What are the top five things you want to do? Even if you don't get round to doing them. (For example, exercise, job hunting, starting a new business, reading.)

1. ....

2. ....

3. ....

4. ....

5. ....

Add the total time spent doing these activities each week:

.... [hours] .... [mins]

Who do you envy, admire, dream of being, want to think or do like? Wanting to be like others distracts us and drains our energy.

1. ....

2. ....

3. ....

4. ....

5. ....

Whenever you do this, you're distracted from focusing on your own brilliance, and how you can bring that to the table.

Complete the following:

I spend .... [hours] .... [mins] doing things that I don't want to do.

I spend .... [hours] .... [mins] doing things that I most want to do.

If procrastination is more than just a troublesome avoidance tactic, you'll be thinking: 'If only it were that easy'. A friend of mine, a self-confessed procrastinator, has recommended *The Now Habit* by Neil Fiore. It has given him strategies for dealing with his procrastination. It talks about some of the same issues we have mentioned above, working in the 'flow state' and overcoming blockers, as well as the concept of 'guilt-free play'. Guilt-free play is based on the apparent paradox that in order to do productive, high quality work on important projects, you must stop putting off living, and engage wholeheartedly in recreation and relaxation. If this sounds interesting, it might be the book for you.

I stand firm in declaring that we don't procrastinate over things that are truly in line with our passion, purpose and vision. If we do procrastinate, we might think they are, but they aren't. We procrastinate over things we 'have' to do or 'think' we have to do. We can employ strategies to help us do the things we have to do, or we can find out what we want to be doing, and do that instead.

What Does Your Heart Say?

Stick with the heart in all important decisions.

– Alex Grant

We live in a mind-centric culture within which we forget to consult our hearts, giving free reign to wild, frazzled emotions without anchor. Many cultures look to the heart as the epicentre of emotions, a higher intelligence, and even the point where spirit and humanity converge. Here in the West most of us don't integrate those ideas in the same way. Our understanding of the heart marginalises it as an organ, or an ideagraph ubiquitous on 14 February.

It is so much more than that. Our heart – possibly the cleverest organ in our body – forms before our brain. As the brain develops, the 'thinking brain' emerges from the 'emotional brain'. It seems we are emotional beings before we are thinking beings. So it's not so hard to believe that our heart has the capacity to heighten intelligence and intuition. Shouldn't we listen to it more?

The heart offers a softer, more intuitive perspective – it tells us how something *feels* – and whether our choices are happy, light and positive, or sad, heavy and negative. Sometimes you can be sure you're making the *right* decision, but it might not *feel* good. This is your heart weighing in on the discussion. Listening to the feedback and deeper yearnings from our heart space is an effective barometer for decisions that we make with our head. Acting from the heart is the key difference between making *sensible* decisions, and making *authentic* ones that are congruent with your passion, purpose and vision.

When you follow your heart and drop your mask a deep sense of contentment arises.

– Ted Grand

My heart never sits on the sidelines – in fact it's as outspoken as my head is. One month into a twelve-month media contract it was already hollering at me on my daily commute. I wasn't listening. So it conspired with the rest of my body: by mid contract I had insomnia, loss of appetite, chronic neck pain and a deep, physical ache within. My heart was in charge and I had to speak my truth. When I sat down to speak with my boss at work, he heard my truth and it was met with gratitude and respect. When you make decisions with your heart, you can be nothing but authentic. Authenticity cuts through the most logic-oriented reasoning. Hands down, every decision I've ever made that was driven by money or another apparently logical metric has never turned out well.

Do you make decisions with your heart or your head? Do you cross check your left-brain decisions with your heart? Do you listen to that deep ache within and act on its voice? If your heart is not consulted, your emotions will let you know so you have the chance to incorporate its intelligence into your decision making.

What kind of decisions do you usually make with your head? Would your heart give you different advice about these decisions?

1.   ....

2.   ....

3.   ....

4. ....

5. ....

6. ....

7. ....

8. ....

9. ....

10. ....

What kind of decisions do you usually make with your heart? Does your head try to dissuade you?

1. ....

2. ....

3. ....

4. ....

5. ....

6. ....

7. ....

8. ....

9. ....

10. ....

Think of an imminent decision (scenario, or project) that you have to make. Let's see what your heart says.

....

How do you make a decision from the heart?

Leza Lowitz shares some simple steps for heart-centred decision making with us. It might help to have someone else read out the steps while you have your eyes closed:

1. Designate some time to yourself and find a quiet, clear, clean space. (Make it beautiful if you so wish.)
2. Sit or lie down comfortably with your eyes closed.
3. Think about the decision you have to make.
4. What are the options?
5. Imagine yourself following through with option A. Picture yourself in that situation. Imagine it in as much detail as possible. How do you feel? Does it light you up? Describe how you feel, either silently or aloud.
6. Now take a deep breath and do the same with option B.
7. Take another deep breath and continue with option C.
8. And so on with each choice, breathing in between.
9. Open your eyes and write down how you feel about each option.
10. Which option(s) has(ve) the most light around it / them? Which option(s) made you feel good, light, happy and positive?

....

This is the choice that your heart is making.

To continue incorporating heart-centred decision making into any aspect of your life, art, and business:

1. Ask yourself which choice will help the most people.

2. Now you can help someone else realise their dream. Think of a friend with a goal or vision, and make a plan to meet them to discuss their dream and action plan.

3. Commit to each other's plans with solid goals and deadlines. The seeds you plant in helping someone else find and realise their dream will ripen in your own dream coming to fruition.

4. When your dream comes true, have a celebration. Make it spectacular, and share it with as many people as possible.

5. Keep helping people realise their own dreams to ensure the continued success of your own venture. The more people you help, the more seeds you plant for your own success to ripen.

What Is Your Body Telling You?

Listen to your inner knowing and use the body as a barometer to this knowledge – find bodywork techniques that support your journey.

– Deborah Richmond

Your body is an effective barometer for what's happening in your life. Can you hear what it is saying? Whether its voice is a soft whisper or a blood curdling scream, our body talks to us to let us know about our mental, emotional and spiritual imbalances. You're so sad that you cry. You're so nervous you feel sick. You're so stressed you feel a weight on your shoulders. Your body gives you regular feedback. What is your body trying to tell you?

Do you have:

- Recurring sore throats or tonsillitis? Are you not speaking your truth?

- Crazy eczema or other skin conditions? Do you feel unsafe or unprotected?

- Problems with your legs? Are you afraid to move forward?

- Digestive issues? What in your life are you having trouble 'digesting'?

- Eye problems? What are you seeing that you just don't like?

- Hearing problems? What are you actively trying not to listen to?

- Lower back pain? Where do you not feel supported?

This list could go on to include each part of your body. For all you sceptics out there, if you really listen, really look deeply, you'll be amazed at the correlations between your body and your experience right now.

If anything is out of whack for me, it's always my neck, signalling either repressed expression, or inflexibility. The neck is the location of the fifth chakra, which represents communication and expression. Prone to tonsillitis or laryngitis when I'm not speaking my truth, I've learned to listen to the pain in my throat and interpret it as encouragement to speak up. This might be my cue to start something, end something, get more information, or re-evaluate.

As a symbol of mental and emotional flexibility, it could also mean I'm being rigid somewhere in my life. In 2012 I had chronic neck pain that required upper cervical treatment, but the condition corrected itself when I followed the calling to leave the corporate world. I realised there was another way to write the book: on the road in Central America.

If you have pain or discomfort, is your body trying to tell you something? Can you start listening more intently?

Your body is your temple. Begin there. Simple things ... start to be more mindful of the food that you put into your body. Candy? Junk food? Processed foods? Sugar? No need to be radical, just become more aware of how much better you feel when you eat less of the above. Read a bit about healthier eating strategies. ...What kind of food am I putting into my body? How am I taking care of this life-giving vessel?

– Charley Patton

One of the easiest and most simple things to do to become aware of the subtle language of your body is to clean it out. This doesn't have to be a full-on detox, although that's good, too (apple, fennel and cucumber juice, YUM!). It simply calls for greater awareness of what you eat, when you eat it, and how it makes you feel.

1. Is your body craving certain things?

2. Is it responding to harmful addictions, or directing your attention to deficiencies?

3. How do chemical additives, drugs, alcohol or nicotine affect your body's language?

4. How could you create a cleaner terrain?

When you ask yourself these sorts of questions, your body can begin to speak to you.

To learn your body's language, first draw two crude outlines of the human body (FBI style) side by side on a piece of scrap paper. Label the one on the left 'front' and the one on the right 'back'. Circle the parts that present pain, stiffness or discomfort, either chronically or acutely. Now you can investigate.

There are multiple sources of information that explain the symbolic relevance of the body, right to down to whether it's your left or right finger. My two favourites are:

• *The Body is The Barometer of the Soul* by Annette Noontil

• *Heal Your Body A–Z* by Louise L. Hay

What are some of the things that might be muting your body's voice? Clue: You don't get addicted to grapes and cucumbers. Think of the foods you crave that might contain chemical substances, hormones or antibiotics (like cheese or bread); recreational or prescription drugs; additives or pesticides; alcohol or tobacco.

Be specific. Pecorino Toscano (a hard Italian cheese made from ewe's milk). Domino's pizza. Chocolate almond croissant. Turkish coffee with one spoon of sugar. American Spirit tobacco.

1. ....

2. ....

3. ....

4. ....

5. ....

6. ....

7. ....

8. ....

9. ....

10. ....

Become aware of why you eat, consume or take them, and how they make your body feel. You can identify patterns and dynamics that affect everything you do (and determine whether what you eat is creative or counter-creative).

What do you typically have for:

• Breakfast:

....

• Lunch:

....

• Dinner:

....

What are your top five (favourite) snacks?

1. ....

2. ....

3. ....

4. ....

5. ....

How could you add more real, fresh, raw, alive foods and drinks to your day? Could you:

• Eat at home?

• Prepare a packed lunch?

• Add a green juice or smoothie before breakfast?

• Have a salad for dinner? Try Meg Worden's Salad Alchemy ('7 lovely life-shifting salads') at http://megworden.com/salad-alchemy

• Shop at local farmers markets or get an organic veggie box deliver to your door once a week?

- Grow your own veggie garden or herbs?
- Cook with your friend or partner?
- Buy a new cookbook for inspiration?

When your body is clean, you can ask it how it feels, listen to what it's telling you and check-in with it regularly.

Chapter 9: Get The Basics in Place

Chapter Snapshot

- Breathe
- Move Your Body
- Find Your Stillness
- Create Space
- Connect with Nature

Breathe

Breathe. Become more conscious of your breath. You can't live without it. Think of your breath as nourishment for every cell in your body ... it's true, do so deeply.

– Charley Patton

We take in over 21,000 breaths every day. Each breath we take fuels our body's vital processes and helps us to produce energy. The right amount of oxygen in our body feeds all of our cells, increases our energy levels, stimulates circulation, balances our energy flow throughout our body, and keeps all of our systems healthy and in check. Optimum health is directly proportionate to the quality of our breath, so becoming aware of it and learning to breathe efficiently is essential.

Given how important it is, why don't they teach us how to breathe at school? We learn maths, physics and chemistry (sex education if we're lucky, skiing if you're in Scandinavia) yet nobody teaches is how to b-r-e-a-t-h-e properly. Although we breathe automatically, we can also use the breath as a tool to improve body-mind health, as well as raise our levels of consciousness. At a physical level, breathing into specific areas of tightness and pain is soothing and therapeutic. At a more mental or emotional level we can use it to balance hyperactivity or depression.

As such, our breath is an accurate barometer for our physical, mental and emotional states:

- It's easier when we're calm and focused.
- It's harder when we're stressed or worried.
- It's faster when we're exercising or excited.
- It's slower when we're relaxed.
- It's deeper when we're meditative.

Tune in to your breath and its quality – the most basic form of awareness of your energy – learning how to use it to enhance health and wellbeing. You'll wish they had taught you to breath at school.

Whenever I feel blue, I start breathing again.

– L. Frank Baum, author of *The Wonderful Wizard of Oz*

Take a few moments to check-in with your breath. Describe its natural quality. Is it short? Shallow? Easy? Deep? Fast? Slow? Is your inhale longer than your exhale? Or vice versa? Is there a gap between your inhale and exhale?

- Inhale .... seconds
- Space in between .... seconds
- Exhale .... seconds

Try this. Inhale for seven seconds, drawing your breath first into your stomach and then up into your chest. Retain it for four seconds, then exhale completely for seven seconds. Do a couple of rounds of this: inhale for seven – retain for four – exhale for seven. Focus on removing irregularities and creating smooth, continuous breathing. What do you notice?

When is your breath irregular? Mental and emotional stress affects the quality of our breath. The more regular your breath, the more energy, vitality and calm you create.

1. ....

2. ....

3. ....

4. ....

5. ....

6. ....

7. ....

8. ....

9. ....

10. ....

In these moments, focus on deepening and balancing your breath to bring you back into your body and to a centred, calm state.

Channel your breath into areas of tightness or pain. I've been doing either one of these two exercises every day since I practised with Richard Holroyd in 2012. Try them when you have a quiet moment to yourself (or just tell everyone to shush).

Exercise 1 – Breathe into your belly

1. Lie flat on your belly, resting your forehead on a pillow formed by overlapping your hands. Your legs should be relaxed, letting your ankles turn out, but not so much that your lower back feels tight.

2. Breathe deeply into your belly and retain for a short period without strain (like you do before sneezing – there's a natural 'moment' of retention before the activity starts again).

3. Notice, in this order, your belly filling, your sides expanding, your lower back lifting.

4. Breathe out for longer than the inhalation if possible (start with counting if you're unsure until you can re-tune into your body's rhythm and begin to trust instinct again).

5. Repeat twenty times.

6. Notice any changes in your mood, the feeling of your body, the length or depth of your breath and the quality of your breath. You might like to select one or two of these 'goals' before starting, otherwise you'll be thinking too much. Alternatively, simply notice any changes in your body, your breath, or your mind as you experience them.

Exercise 2 – Breathe into your back

1. Kneel with your knees separated enough for the sitz bone to be close to the heels. (If uncomfortable place a blanket between your heels and sitz bone – or just toughen up!)

2. Your arms can be extended forward (if this is not uncomfortable for the shoulders), or placed by the side of your feet.

3. Your forehead must be supported by the floor or a prop (like a blanket), ensuring that the base of your neck feels no strain.

4. Sit with your legs folded beneath you, stretching your arms forward and resting your forehead on the ground.

5. Breathe deeply into your back (top, middle, bottom), and retain for a short period without strain (like you do before sneezing; there's a natural 'moment' of retention before the activity starts again).

6. Notice – in this order – the contact between your expanding belly against your inner thigh, the flaring out of side of your ribs, the rising up of your chest and collarbones. This is called *the flowering of the heart centre.*

7. Repeat twenty times.

8. Notice any changes in your mood, the feeling of your body, the length or depth of your breath and the quality of your breath? You might like to select one or two of these 'goals' before starting, otherwise you'll be thinking too much. Alternatively, simply notice any changes in your body, your breath, or your mind as you experience them.

Move Your Body

When you stop moving... you stop moving.

– Anna Laurita

'Move your body' should be the second mantra of your waking moments. In fact, it should be written on Post-its and stuck on your bedside table, bathroom mirror, toilet door, kitchen counter and front door. When we move our body we transform static energy into vibrancy in seconds.

When we don't move our body, it's not just our body that stops moving; everything stagnates. You feel weak and lethargic, perhaps even a little 'compacted' or 'blobby' (like after sitting at your desk all day, or on a plane for eighteen hours). Moving (walking, swimming, running, or even the cheekiest of stretches) increases blood flow to the brain and body and, suddenly, woooohoooo! Motivation. Inspiration. Enthusiasm. You're unstoppable. You expand in all directions as energy and vitality flow through your veins delivering organic voltage to every cell in your body (and you thought that red stuff was just blood). Movement creates flexibility in our muscles, bones and ligaments, and opens us up to the more subtle movement of energy flow in our body.

Inhale deeply and learn to touch your toes.

– Aimee Hartley

Movement is one of those things we resist, yet when we do it, we feel absolutely fabulous. We're least likely to move when we feel stagnant or depressed, simply because we lack the energy, but movement creates the energy we lack. Resistance to movement can mean that:

- Your body is trying to protect itself, due to injury or the real need for rest.
- You are trapped in the impossible downward spiral of laziness.
- You're in a comfort zone that requires breaking through self-imposed judgements and limitations ('I need to lose weight before I go to the gym').

Identifying the cause of your resistance to movement will enable you to either:

1. Rest
2. Move your ass

Ask yourself: 'Am I tired, or do I feel stagnant?'

Body Language:

Tired = 'Rest'

Stagnant = 'Move your ass'

I think we all have days where we wake up feeling tired and stagnant. Most days stretching helps to release energy, and doing something like yoga or running can really help to energise us. Other days it's really important to rest. If you 'collapse' after stretching, or feel light-headed or dizzy, you're pushing yourself too hard. Rest. When you're well rested you can begin with gentle forms of exercise and then move to something more dynamic as you build up your strength. We benefit from movement when it's incremental.

I start every day by sitting up in bed and checking in. I ask, *How do I feel?* I drink a glass of water. *How do I feel?* I head to the kitchen for a protein shake. *How do I feel?* I head off for my walk. *How do I feel?* I fall into a gentle jog. *How do I feel?* If I feel great I keep running. I push a little, just to the edge, but back off if I need to. Check in with yourself constantly. Listen to your body and what it's telling you.

Develop your own knowledge, wisdom and vision for your body, and how movement can benefit it:

Knowledge = If I move I'll feel better.

Wisdom = Jogging and boot camp sets my energy free, and yoga and meditation helps me channel it into a physical and spiritual feeling of expansion.

Vision = My body is a strong, balanced, intelligent home for my mind, heart and spirit.

Now it's your turn. How does movement 'work' for you?

Knowledge = ...

Wisdom = ...

Vision = ...

What are some of your beliefs and associations surrounding movement?

1. Grab a large piece of paper and write 'movement' in the centre. Create a mind map, plotting everything that comes into your mind when you think about movement. Give yourself five minutes, and don't stop writing. Include both positive and negative associations.

2. Circle what you consider to be the main motivations and / or blocks when it comes to movement. (For some, movement is 'effort'; for others, movement is 'play').

Start your day with 'rag doll'. Raphan Kebe's rag doll is my favourite. He's shared it with us here:

1. Standing with your feet underneath your sitz bone (directly below your hips), softly bend your knees and fold into a forward bend.

2. Take hold of opposite elbows and, while keeping your feet flat, rock your body from side to side by bending your knees one after the other.

3. Release your hands down, move your head as if to say 'yes'.

4. Move your head as if to say 'no'.

5. Then 'maybe'.

6. Once again, bend your knees one after the other, while relaxing your neck and shoulders.

7. Start rolling up one vertebrae at a time by pushing through the right foot as you bend the right knee and pushing through the left foot as you bend the left knee.

8. The neck stays relaxed throughout and the head is the last body part to 'stack up'.

9. Pushing through both feet, lift your arms up while the shoulders roll down.

10. Exhale: '*Namaste*'. (The literal meaning of *Namaste* is a greeting, meaning 'I bow to you' but it also conveys love, respect and humility.)

11. Keeping your hands together, soften your knees slightly to the point where you might feel them wobble.

12. Lengthen the back of your neck, relax your shoulders and your tummy, and let your body's weight travel all the way down, down through your legs, through your feet and on to the floor.

13. Close your eyes and allow the floor to eventually 'push' you back up.

14. Breathe normally; there is no need to either control or manipulate the breath.

15. Open your eyes and be aware of your environment, noticing any change in your appreciation for the space in and around you. Yes! You *are it* and *part of it*.

Commit to regular movement:

- **Beg, steal, or borrow.** A bike, a kayak, a skateboard.

- **Sign up for online coupon deals.** There are great monthly offers and unlimited passes and ideas for all sorts of ways to move. Nothing is more motivating than free or inexpensive ways to move your body.

- **Get someone to move with you.** Arrange to meet someone you don't live with. Walk, run, cycle, etc., even if it's just to the coffee shop (or the pub, or whatever).

- **Join skate or bike night.** In cities all around the world, skaters and bikers claim the streets as their own on certain nights of the week. Get kitted out and join in!

Find Your Stillness

Slow down. Close your eyes and be quiet.

– Silla Siebert

Do you ever feel your life is in a constant state of fast forward? Too frazzled to sit still because there's so much to do? Far too busy to do nothing? We do ourselves a disservice, because ah-ha moments are born in stillness. Stillness comes from slowing down, paying attention to what we're doing, and cultivating a more mindful approach to any activity. When we are *still* we encounter our own inner world without distraction. When we become really good at this, we can develop a mindful state of non-doing (doing nothing). This is called *meditation*.

The easiest way to begin to encounter our own inner world for the first time is to do something we love. When we are immersed in these activities, external distractions and mental chatter fade away. Our minds become quieter and more still as we become lost in the moment. These are activities that absorb 120 per cent of our attention.

If we can step to the side of the 'more, more, more' culture – the 'bigger, better, faster' culture – what we will find is the quiet, still and calm, the de-cluttered mental and physical space to let go. To soften and connect to what is really important.

– Katie Manitsas

I have always struggled with classic forms of meditation, but meditation through movement benefits my mind and my body. When hiking I'm surrounded by such natural beauty that my mind is full of only wonder and birdsong. In high altitude all thoughts are silenced as you focus on your breath. Kayaking is a full body experience as you focus on the rhythm of your stroke and the ache of your muscles over long distances. When swimming I focus only on the lap number. In yoga I focus on the quality of my breath or my alignment within the posture. Physical activities can be a great way to encounter the edges of stillness for the first time.

By silencing external distractions and mental chatter we can experience quiet. In this quiet our mind can be still. A still mind is a happy mind.

You can immerse yourself in the physical experience of anything – it really doesn't matter what you do. You just have to give it 120 per cent of your attention. You could:

- Walk around the block, counting your steps.

- Make a smoothie, mindful of each movement involved.

- Eat a mango, savouring every bite.

- Sit under a tree, gaze at the branches and the flecks of sky in-between.

- Sit on a bench and breath. Inhale. Exhale. (Listen to: Shpongle's 'Nothing is Something Worth Doing').

Everything takes time. Bees have to move very fast to stay still.

 – David Foster Wallace, *Brief Interviews with Hideous Men*

You can turn any part of your day into an opportunity to be still:

- Listen to an audio book on your commute.

- Take a few deep breaths while waiting for the lift.

- Savour your cup of Earl Grey tea, sip by sip.

- Sit in your favourite reading chair with a good book.

What physical activities command 120 per cent of your attention?

1. ....

2. ....

3. ....

4. ....

5. ....

What activities silence external distraction and mental chatter? (Cooking, gardening, other hobbies.)

1. ....

2. ....

3. ....

4. ....

5. ....

What routine tasks characterise your day? (Making your bed, eating breakfast, getting dressed, walking to the station.) Rather than rushing, could you bring more 'mindfulness' to them?

1. ....

2. ....

3. ....

4. ....

5. ....

Chanoyu, the name given to the Japanese Tea Ceremony, is considered one way of experiencing inner stillness, owing to the ritual and repetition involved in preparing, serving and drinking tea.

A ritual that spans centuries, young men and women in Japan take *Chanoyu* lessons in order to learn traditional Japanese etiquette. It has also become popular with foreigners, too, who study it to experience the serenity, order and peaceful calm instilled by the experience.

Create Space

There is freedom in space.

– Holly Coles

As we dedicate ever more time to activities that generate stillness, our lives become more spacious. We can continue to expand that sense of space both on the inside – mentally, emotionally and spiritually – and on the outside.

Breathing exercises and other types of meditation expand our feelings of spaciousness on the inside, because they kick monkey mind to the curb. But it needn't be as complicated as a formal practice; it can be as simple as paying greater attention to the quality of your breath.

As you surrender to a physical expansion on the inhale, and a letting go on the exhale, you notice that thoughts, feelings and other sensations arise. This is your deep Self speaking to you, and the longer you allow this to happen, the more acquainted with your Self you become, though it can seem like a stranger at first.

It takes the time and space to observe your own thoughts and figure out what it is that you're manifesting.

– Lawrence Quirk

You might be wondering what space feels like and how you can create more of it.

For a simple experiment to create space in your mind, try this exercise from Gaia. Do it by yourself, or have someone read it to you so you can keep your eyes closed:

1. Find a comfortable cross-legged or other seated position.

2. Allow your eyes to close.

3. Feel your seat anchored to the ground and allow the crown of your head to feel as if it's being lifted.

4. Sit up straight, lengthen your spine and tuck your chin in slightly.

5. Soften your shoulders, your hips and your jaw.

6. Become aware of your breath as it moves in and out of your nostrils.

7. Deepen your breath, inviting it into the entire chest cavity: bottom, top, front, back, right and left.

8. Continue to be aware of your breath, accepting any thoughts, feelings and sensations that arise.

9. Feel for the expansion that happens on the inhale and the sense of letting go on the exhale.

10. Notice what is present in you. This is space. This is expansion.

If you were to practice this breathing exercise three times a week at first, working your way to a daily practice, you would become more comfortable with the space you encounter. Chances are it might expand into your daily experience, noticeable in a more relaxed approach to everything. However, there is a caveat to its effectiveness. If your physical world is characterised by chaos, its potential to expand into your real-world experience will be thwarted. Pretty much like Buzz Lightyear's quest to reach infinity and beyond.

Clutter and untidiness can cause stress and anxiety, reversing the best laid intentions.

Creating the right conditions on the outside can help the inner terrain align much more easily. As soon as we tidy up our real-world spaces we can progress to more advanced states of spaciousness (mental, emotional and spiritual). Real-world spaces are the physical locations where you live, work and play, and include anywhere you happen to find yourself during the day. Think of the spaces where you:

- Sleep

- Eat

- Relax

- Exercise

- Meditate

- Work

- Commute

My bedroom and bathroom are sacred spaces. I keep them spotless and free of digital devices. I clean my work space at the end of each day, spritz it with essential oils and buy fresh flowers once a week. During my last contract I found the rush-hour commute stressful, so I got up an hour earlier to avoid the crowds. I run through parkland or on beaches because I find gyms over-subscribed. There are so many simple ways to make our physical spaces happy, spacious places.

Maintaining quality physical space is a really great way of welcoming more advanced levels of spaciousness into your life. It's like saying, 'I'm ready for more space. Bring it on!'

Believe it or not, our day is full of natural space. It feels empty, so our instinct is to fill it, perhaps with smoking, eating or drinking, or perhaps with social media or work. When you encounter these moments, see them as an opportunity to create space. They might be intimidating or uncomfortable, but try focusing on your breath and maybe even closing your eyes for a moment to transform them. Rather than filling them, try to expand that space actively. Tap into the sensory experience of being alive.

How to create one hour of space every day

1. Focus on the quality of your breath for twenty mins.

2. Move for twenty mins.

3. Be still for twenty mins.

How to create fourteen hours of space each week

• Take the above exercise and double it.

Breathe, move, be still, clean up, tidy up, and de-clutter, and prepare to tap into infinity and beyond.

Japanese Gardens are created so that the visitor can recognise a sense of peace, tranquillity and harmony. Core elements used in the design of every Japanese Garden are stones, water, and plants, which represent landscape, life force, and the four seasons. As a visitor, you're included as part of the environment, and can acknowledge yourself as an integral part of the universe through the human scale of the garden – you're never overpowered by it. It's a space for serenity and escaping the rigmarole of day-to-day life.

Connect with Nature

The earth is an amazing place, with its own natural intelligence. The same intelligence that made you. You are nature. Connect with it.

– Charley Patton

Remember the scene in *Pretty Woman* where Vivian (Julia Roberts) drags Edward (Richard Gere) – busy corporate type – to the park, takes off his shoes, and plants his feet in the grass? She instinctively knew that he needed some nature. When was the last time you broke up your day with your feet in the grass, listening to the birds sing? Or strolled to the local pond and shrieked with delight as the edges of the ice cracked beneath your feet? Or watched fruit bats sleeping upside down in the botanical gardens? If you're not actively connecting with nature, you're disconnected from its natural intelligence. If you're disconnected from nature's natural intelligence, you can't tap into it.

If you don't connect with nature daily, most likely you've lost touch with its amazing-ness. Connecting to it feels so good. Imagine:

- The flow of a river current over your feet.

- Your feet buried in the sand at the edge of the ocean.

- Showering under a waterfall in the jungle.

- Standing in the rain.

- Lying in the grass looking up at the sky.

- Your whole body immersed in mud.

- Sleeping in a hammock under the stars listening to the ocean roar.

While, supposedly, only three per cent of the earth's surface comprises urban jungle, half the entire global population lives in it[12]. In the cities we might have to seek it out, but there is always a blade of grass, potted plant or fountain somewhere. Find it. Sit next to it. Look at it. Listen to it. Meditate on it.

Entrepreneurs and government funding are making it easier for urban folk to experience more open space. With the rise of urban green space projects in major capital cities around the world, and scientific research that proves it's good for us, it shouldn't be too long before some urban greenery comes to an urban jungle near you, too.

A new study in Psychological Science reveals that the benefits of urban green space – and the more of it, the better – extend far beyond the purely ornamental. Increases in green space correspond to increases in happiness, decreases in depression, and a general bump to well-being and life satisfaction.

– Maria Konnikova, 'Want to Be Happier and Live Longer? Protect Green Spaces', Scientific American[13]

Greenery is becoming the centrepiece of urban development projects around the world. James Corner, the architect of New York City's High Line Park, wanted to create a *'secret, magic garden in the sky'*, and underneath Manhattan's Lower East Side a group of entrepreneurs have proposed to create a space filled with natural light and foliage (supposedly the size of an American football field).[14]

Our natural craving for greenery and the desire to create it has spawned a wave of start-ups to satisfy our demand for more of it. ALLOTINABOX[15] design 'grow your own boxes' that enable anyone to grow wherever they are. So if you fancy a bit more green in your life, buy a basil plant or turn your room into an urban jungle with something potted.

Write down the exact day/month/year you:

- Felt the earth/dirt/mud/sand/grass beneath your bare feet.

....

- Sat out at night and gazed at the stars.

....

- Watched the sunset or sunrise.

....

- Danced in the rain.

....

- Walked in a park / hiked through a forest, wood or national park / climbed a mountain / trekked the desert.

....

- Hung out with or snuggled a cute critter: cat / dog / turtle / mountain lion.

....

- Scheduled nature time in your calendar.

....

Which of these things got your juices flowing when you read it? Circle it. Commit to doing this one thing at least once a week, and declare:

I .... [insert name] believe that the earth is an amazing place, and dedicate ....
.... [insert hrs : mins] to .... [insert activity] to get my body and mind closer to nature so that I can plug into its innate intelligence.

Enjoy the wilderness. Every prophet has to spend some time out there ... and know that the universe supports your every move as it patiently directs you to the place where you can make your contribution to the grand evolution of life.

– Richard Holroyd

Chapter 10: Unleash Your Core Qualities

Chapter Snapshot

- Be Kind
- Be Truthful
- Be Brave
- Be Empowered
- Be Creative
- Discover Your Innate Talents

Be Kind

Be loving and kind to oneself, and all of life, all of the time, no matter what.

– David Sye

If there were no comparisons, kindness would be effortless. But we want to be thinner, more fit, more beautiful. We want to be smarter, more successful, better paid. We want to be more qualified, better spoken and better dressed. 'More than' who? Who sets the benchmark? Being kind is leaving the desire to be 'more than' behind and focusing on loving and appreciating yourself as you are. Are you kind to yourself in every moment of your aliveness?

We live with expectations of meteoric proportions. Others might set them, but we perpetuate them. They can be so lofty and idealistic that only a demi-god could possibly live up to them (and even they would have had the wrath of the gods to contend with before certain victory).

From the dimples on the back of our thighs to plumping our lips with Botox; from botching up a presentation to not applying for a pay-rise; from screwing up a relationship to wondering why our libido is lower than that of our favourite TV character; from forcing ourselves out of bed when we know we need to rest to staying in a job we hate, we beat ourselves up as we continue to compare, contrast, and keep up.

Wouldn't it be great if kindness were an in-built default mechanism? What if you said, 'I love and respect myself. What is the kindest thing I can do, say and think for myself right now?' In our quest to improve ourselves, we often bypass the only metric that ever really matters: kindness.

How do we learn to be more kind to ourselves? How do we become more compassionate, more gentle and more loving?

Living a naked, natural life taught me to give myself permission to follow the little voice inside. I guided myself towards the wisdom of the earth. I have learned to trust, to be kind, and to be compassionate with myself.

– Gaia

Kindness *is* an in-built default mechanism, but sadly in our culture of bigger, better, more, the instinctive voice of our 'deep self' is drowned out by the rallying cries of the media and the status quo which usurp the sweet utterings of our noble hearts.

At first, it takes concerted effort to bathe ourselves in compassion, but when we do, we sink into it, discover stillness, expand into our space, and allow our experience to unfold. We can begin to exist unfettered by all the stories that cloud our judgment. Kindness-to-self becomes unapologetic and unbridled, and we extend it to others more authentically.

In Sanskrit, the word for kindness is *ahimsa*, meaning 'doing no harm'. It has three aspects:

1. Actions
2. Words
3. Thoughts

To be kind to yourself and others you need only ask yourself whether your actions, words and thoughts are causing no harm.

Kindness-to-self checklist. Are you:

1. Listening? What does your body, mind, heart, or spirit need at this very moment? (Rest, inspiration, love, or space?) Be fully present to your needs.

2. Allowing? Can you allow yourself just to 'be', and accept fully *who* you are and *what* you are in this very moment?

3. Trusting? Can you trust that each and every experience is part of an evolutionary journey of your life? You're exactly where you're meant to be.

Kindness-to-others Checklist. Are you:

1. Being kind to yourself? If you are loving and kind to yourself, can you treat others with pure, unadulterated kindness.

2. Listening? Are you fully present to their needs in this moment? Sometimes kindness is no more than listening with care and attention.

3. Being happy, positive and humorous? Joy and love nurture the heart of humanity, no matter what the situation. In *La Vita è Bella*, Guido (Roberto Benigni) imagines that the Holocaust is a game and the grand prize for winning is a tank. How can you bring kindness to transform someone's perspective?

What do you do, say or think when you see:

• A stranger crying on a bench in the street?
• A homeless person sleeping in a stairwell?
• A child begging for scraps or spare change?
• A spider in the bath?
• A bee flailing in your glass of water?
• Litter on the pavement?

(Kindness can also be extended to animals and the planet.)

What random act of kindness could you perform today?

• Smile at a stranger.
• Help someone pack their groceries.
• Bake someone a cake (back to those chocolate cupcakes...).
• Buy someone a coffee.
• Have a conversation with a homeless person (buy them a sandwich).

Kindness questions:

What do you frequently apologise for? (Body, behaviours, actions)

1. ....

2. ....

3. ....

4. ....

5. ....

What do you frequently beat yourself up over? (Body, behaviours, actions)

1. ....

2. ....

3. ....

4. ....

5. ....

What kindness do you extend to others and not yourself?
Where do you give others the benefit of the doubt, and bathe
them in love and compassion? Think of the physical, emotional, mental and spiritual aspects of your actions and gestures, as well as your behaviours and characteristics.

1. ....

2. ....

3. ....

4. ....

5. ....

Mini self-kindness exercises

- **Shower yourself with love and compassion.** Step outside
yourself for a moment and see yourself as a person beating themselves up or apologising about something. Feel
love and compassion for them. Visualise them showered
in love and compassion. Bring in the pink hearts or pink
glow, or a giant, warm, furry bear hug. Then give yourself
one. And get one from someone else. (This works, too!)

- **Imagine yourself as a five-year-old.** Close your eyes and imagine your five-year-old self in front of you. They are sad or crying. Tell them it's OK. Tell them the most important thing is to love and respect themselves. Reach out your arms and give them a great big giant hug. Feel the love and kindness flow from you to them, and right back to you again. Feel the sadness melt and kindness flood your body.

- **Ask yourself: 'Why am I being so hard on myself?'** What have I got to prove? Who am I trying to impress? Why is this a reason to be unkind to myself? Why am I trying to compare, contrast or keep up?

- **Ask yourself, 'What is the kindest thing I can do, say or think for myself right now?'.** Stand still for a moment and focus on your breath. Breathe in love and compassion. Gently ask yourself, 'What is the next step?' From that place you can move forward and handle the situation with kindness for yourself and others.

In the Yoga Sūtras, kindness (ahimsa) comes before truthfulness (satya). When you propose to speak, follow that order.

– Lauren Peterson

Truth is up next.

Ahimsa finds its way into the bedrock of start-ups mentioned in Chapter 4. Not only are they profitable businesses supporting the passion and purpose of the founders and employees alike (kindness to Self), but they are also living, breathing statements of what is wrong in the world and visions of how much better the world could be (kindness to Others). By acting as a force for social good, these entrepreneurs demonstrate that businesses can comprise kind, global citizens that strive to bring equality to humanity and healing to the planet.

Be Truthful

The only thing that actually makes a real difference is to accept – and by that I mean pay attention to and make space for (with an open body and mind) – what is actually happening NOW and what you are, and what you think you are, NOW.

– Charlotte Carnegie

Truth can flourish where there is kindness because when bathed in love and compassion we feel safe. We're armed to face the brutal truth – the truth of who we are and where we're at *right now*.

In Sanskrit the word for truth is *satya*, which roughly translates as 'unchangeable', meaning constant or absolute. The root word – *sat* – means 'to be'. It is unchangeable because it is simply the truth of what 'is' (otherwise known as 'reality'). If you can acknowledge the reality of *who* you are and *what* you are right now, you can realise your furthest potential and unfurl your brilliance across the universe. Hoorah!

When you acknowledge the who, what, where, why and how with truth and clarity, you make way for a clear path to your ultimate vision. Being and accepting who you are – rather than pretending to be someone else – will propel you along your path at breakneck speed. Hurdles become checkpoints to make sure you check-in with your truth regularly.

I learned to get really naked. I mean totally bare, raw and vulnerable, open to all possibilities and realisations. I learned to accept myself and the dance of life, even the horrible bits.

– Gaia

Self-acceptance is liberating. In acknowledging our most loathsome parts we can explore how they serve us and learn how and where we demonstrate their opposite traits. We are, in fact, the perfect blend of every available trait, and all of them serve us in some way. How does Chapter 2 of Lao-Tzu's *Tao Te Ching* begin? With the recognition that since beauty exists, so too does ugliness. Opposites define each other; you cannot be bitchy without also being respectful. You cannot be arrogant without also being humble. You cannot be rude without also being polite. You cannot be unreliable without also being reliable *in some area of your life*. Opposites give each other meaning and demonstrate that we exist in a perfect state of duality.

I'm impetuous, fickle and opinionated. By accepting and allowing those parts, and not sweeping them under the proverbial carpet, I have greater awareness of who I really am. Somehow it allows those traits to soften and collaborate with my best self (after all, I am fast-acting, flexible, and articulate), and I also become aware of the flip side of those traits and where I demonstrate them, because I can also be reflective, constant and open-minded.

I call this exercise 'Truth Without Tears'

What are your top three loathsome traits? How do they serve you and what are their opposing traits? Use the *Opposite Word Calculator* (http://www.opposite-word.com).

Loathsome Trait No. 1: ....

1. How does it serve you?
2. What is its opposing trait?

3. Where in your life do you demonstrate it?

Loathsome Trait No. 2: ....

1. How does it serve you?
2. What is its opposing trait?
3. Where in your life do you demonstrate it?

Loathsome Trait No. 3: ....

1. How does it serve you?
2. What is its opposing trait?
3. Where in your life do you demonstrate it?

You don't have to disown your loathsome traits.

- **Own** them, loud and proud!
- **Acknowledge** how they serve you.
- **Witness** how they transform in different areas of your life.

Where are my achievements, my knowledge, my ambitions, my wealth, my success, or my beliefs right at this moment? None of them are a part of the present moment; they're all just abstractions, mental concepts which you have to think into existence. All you are and all you have at this present moment is your awareness – of your own being and of your surroundings.

– Steve Taylor, author of Out of The Darkness: From Turmoil to Transformation

We are a label-centric lot: daughter, son, marketing director, mother, father, yogi, therapist, architect, spiritual guru, rich, poor, author, CEO, footballer, student, editor, writer, artist, the list goes on. But if you strip away all these titles, all this inflated word play, you are who you are. No more and no less.

We hide ourselves under layers of make-up, aftershave, clothes, labels and brands. Who lies underneath all of that? Who might that person be? You. What lies beneath all those layers is your pure, unadulterated Self.

Who are you when you strip away all the titles, labels, brands, clothing and make-up? Who are you right here, right now?

....

....

....

....

....

Get naked. Expose your most raw, vulnerable, physical Self. For Gaia, getting naked is about sharing your soul, and she believes physical nudity can be a stepping-stone to that experience.

1. Stand naked in front of a mirror, both feet flat on the ground.

2. From your toes to the top of your head, tell the story of your body and your relationship with it. Aloud, describe scars, oddities, birthmarks. Mention five parts you love and say why. Mention five parts you dislike and say why. Describe, in simple language, what you see. Notice what memories surface. Be present to emotion that arises. This is your body. This is your story.

3. (Optional) Invite your partner to share what they see. Ask them what they love about your body.

Step 3 teaches you how you are seen by others. By bringing your attention to what they see and love about you, strength and acceptance emerge from your truth and theirs. As you embrace the story of your life through your body, you develop a respect for the incredible home it provides for your spirit and your experience of life. You will come to treat it with greater love and kindness.

Be Brave

Sometimes you have to close your eyes and jump – indecision or anxiety about a transformation (after doing all of the research) can be paralysing. I have always had success in closing my eyes and jumping at that point.

– Anna Laurita

Fear is a gift of aliveness and the voice of our inner sage, something for which we can be grateful. Being brave is a decision to confront fear and listen to what it is telling you. It can be both a warning of danger and reassurance you that you're going the right way.

Fear is multidimensional:

1. It can magnify your feeing of aliveness. Take base jumping in a volcano, for example. You could die. You could be injured. The greater the fear, the greater the thrill, the greater the feeling of aliveness.

2. It can protect us from danger. Call it survival instinct, whether there is a real physical danger or just a feeling that something is not right, fear is our knowing or intuition guiding us to back off, do something different, or get more information before proceeding.

3. It characterises the first step out of the comfort zone. Stepping out of our comfort zone can be terrifying. In expanding our experience of life we may face resistance. This kind of fear beckons exploration and a sense of adventure.

How do we identify which kind of fear we are facing? We confront and listen. It can consume every thought in your mind and occupy every cell of your body like the enemy during occupation, but if we face it and hear what it has to say it can be a source of knowledge and wisdom that magnifies our aliveness and helps decision making.

Fear is your body-mind barometer that measures the rightness of a situation, and bravery in the face of it is more than the chivalrous act of putting yourself in front of a bullet. There are many ways to be brave:

1. Confronting fear so you can evaluate it and make a decision about it.

2. Seeing fear as an opportunity for introspection and personal growth.

3. Saying 'yes'.

4. Saying 'no'.

5. Following your own inner compass rather than what others think or say.

6. Asking for help.

7. Helping others.

8. Being kind and truthful.

Of course you can always put yourself in front of the bullet, too. (But what would be the point of that?)

Bravery is a choice that requires evaluation. There is no need to be brave for the sake of it. If you're consumed with full-body paralysis (loss of appetite, insomnia, illness) this mind-body barometer is warning you to proceed with caution, so being a martyr will not benefit you – remember to follow your own inner compass. Fear is part of your body's vocabulary; learn to decipher the different ways it expresses it.

Settle with uncertainty. NOT knowing is a big part of life.

– Silla Siebert

If you want to make a huge life change and are terrified of doing so, congratulations! It is officially confirmed: you are human. Will you succeed? Who knows! But will you start? Lack of certainty can be paralysing. We can write business plans and book plans until we're blue in the face, but their real value is as templates that we fill with detail along the way. They do not provide certainty of success. They do not prevent things from going 'tits up'. Sometimes, the only way to confront your paralysis is to close your eyes and jump. Combat uncertainty with its arch enemies: going with the flow, and trust.

As we go with the flow and allow things to unfold, new ideas, information and opportunities emerge from the unstructured space we've created by taking a risk. Leaving a few unconnected dots allows them to be connected in new, unexpected ways not imagined at the outset. I did not know what form this book would take; it unfurled itself towards my vision as any story would, page by page. I had no idea what it would look like, or that I would leave my job in order to write it (on the road in Mexico, Nicaragua, Oregon and California). The vision was larger than the book itself, allowing the book and the process of writing it to be whatever it needed to be in order to fulfil that vision. It scared the shit out of me.

Sometimes when you're not quite there yet, acting as if you are can create the condition you are seeking.

– Lauren Peterson

Yes, you could be richer, smarter, taller and thinner; you could have more time and money; conditions could always be better ... or could they? Might the biggest risk be to wait for impossibly perfect conditions? Leaning into our edge as we strive towards perfection allows the perfect experience to unfold.

What are you not doing because it seems a bit (or very) scary? Describe it:

1. ....

2. ....

3. ....

4. ....

5. ....

Then consider these next steps:

Choose to be brave. It can be a choice – not just a response.

Say out loud: *Bravery is a choice, and I CHOOSE IT! I choose to be brave!*

Evaluate your fear. Listen to it and hear what it's saying. What are the fears behind the fears? What's the value or belief supporting the fear? If you're afraid of running out of money, what's the real fear behind that? Living on the street? Losing your home? Losing your family? What's the fear behind that? That you are not loved, not supported, not worthy? What's the fear behind that? That you don't believe in yourself? Hunt down the fears behind the fears.

1. ....

2. ....

3. ....

4. ....

5. ....

Who does this fear belong to? Other people mean well, but sometimes it's their own fear they are protecting you from. Did your parents tell you that you should always have three months savings in the bank, no matter what? Did your teachers tell you that if you fail you're useless? Take a look at whose fears this fear is supporting.

1. ....

2. ....

3. ....

4. ....

5. ....

Reframe your perspective. Use it as an opportunity to grow rather than shrink. Will confronting this fear help you grow?

YES / NO

Ask for more information. You might not have all the pieces yet. Can you fill in some gaps before you proceed and be open to filling the rest in as you go?

1. ....

2. ....

3. ....

4. ....

5. ....

Get on with it. See what you are presented with. You can tweak or modify along the way. First, see where it takes you. When can you start? Can you start right now?

YES / NO

Friends tell me repeatedly that I am fearless. I am brave, but not fearless. Being brave is not the same as being fearless. I'm terrified all the time! I love the challenge of confronting the fear and choosing to be brave in spite of it. When you reach the other side your world feels bigger. Expansion occurs and you have more space. Like a Russian doll, you're breaking out of all those layers you exist behind.

Be Empowered

Our edge is a potent opportunity for growth. We will come face to face with ourselves. We may feel a burning desire to make a choice that feels safe just to maintain the status quo.

– Chris Calarco

All the projects, relationships, decisions that we encounter bring us face to face with our loathsome character traits and emotional demons as we wade deeper into those experiences. We see exit signs highlighted in every seedy stairwell and dark cob-webbed corner, beckoning us into a game of Snakes and Ladders. Do you shrink back and slide down, or expand and move forward? Life is not a game. It's a one-time limited-edition experience. Encountering what we consider weakness is an opportunity to transform it into strength.

Our loathsome traits aren't buried very deep. In fact we might meet them almost every day. Almost every role I played in the media world presented me with opportunities to inspire and educate, create new systems, and imbue others with passion, excitement and enthusiasm. On the flip side, the landscape was a breeding ground for my stubbornness, impatience and candidness. Eventually I learned how to filter them; to use their power without their *bite*. Stubbornness transformed into tenacity (to explore all possibilities). Impatience transformed into perseverance (to get the job done). Candidness transformed into compassion (to befriend and inspire). I went from operating in *shadow* to operating in *light*.

Our wounded places are our magic places where all transformation begins.

– Sianna Sherman

Further into the experience (the project, relationship or decision), the stuff that's buried deeper will surface. Emotional demons (like self-doubt and self-loathing) taunt us as they bob to the surface (like the coffins in *Poltergeist*). Help! Get me out of here!

I have a long-held belief that everyone (else) is unreliable – I am radically independent because I would rather stick pins in my eyes than rely on other people. Somehow, contrary to all in-built logic, I embarked on a project that sought contributions from forty-nine people around the world, and reviews from friends and acquaintances as part of the 'indie author' self-publishing process. That's a lot of people to rely on. *Gulp*. The project has not helped me to overcome this belief. On the contrary, it has crystallised it, but I have gained a new insight into what lies behind it (the fear behind the fear): the fear of rejection.

This little insight took me on a journey of self-realisation. Beyond the blistering ache of rejection I discovered the strength that emerges from vulnerability, and the bravery required in asking for help. As I continued to rely on others to help me finish this project, the fear of rejection challenged me to explore: 'How else can I do this? Who else might be able to help me? What happens if I just 'wait'?' It has stoked my creative fires. It has unearthed patience that I never knew I had.

This is the transformative potential of the power of your loathsome traits and emotional demons: self-discovery and exploration. Don't shy away from it. Lean in.

What are your strengths that you notice consistently emerging through your relationships or projects?

....

....

....

What are the 'loathsome' traits that consistently emerge through relationships or projects?

....

....

....

....

....

Can you think of how to transform them in a way that will demonstrate the true value and quality of what you have to offer? You can use Opposite Word Calculator (http://www. opposite-word.com) to flip their meaning and explore where you demonstrate those traits, too.

What are the emotional demons that emerge through relationships or other projects? Fear, self-doubt, self-blame, anger, etc.

....

....

....

What are they trying to tell you or teach you? Do you notice that you're attracted to people, projects, roles, businesses and ideas that present you with the opportunity to confront them? ....

YES / NO

What opportunities do they present?

....

....

....

Be Creative

When you work on something that you are attracted to, your natural creativity to design, problem-solve or manage can emerge regardless of whether it's what is traditionally regarded as a creative industry or not.

– Jyoti Morningstar

The words 'artist' and 'creative' are widely used as nouns and imply someone in a specific artistic field. They should be used more often as adverbs – to describe how you do something. That way more people would know that being artistic is not a rare gift or a profession, but – in more abstract terms – a lens through which we view the world that is available to everyone. If everything we do can be characterised as either 'creative' or 'counter-creative' then *anything* can be done creatively, and anyone can be creative. Yet how many times have you said to yourself, 'I'm just not very creative'?

There's no such thing as creative people and non-creative people. Yes, some of us have an obvious 'raw' talent, but the rest of us have the same potential for unlimited creativity as soon as we discover what our innate talent is.

- Step 1: Find your passion.
- Step 2: Discover your innate talents.
- Step 3: Explore your creativity.

From the moment we're born, we're innately creative. It's another gift of our 'aliveness'.

- **As a baby** we twist and turn our body into so many different shapes; we are boundless natives with our flexibility.
- **At pre-school** we attempt to fit round pegs into square holes, already demonstrating an organic, heart-centred rebellion.
- **At school** we are drawing and painting the world the way we feel it and see it: the sky is pink and the grass is orange. Creativity does not need to be establishment-approved or have commercial value. (So what if your mum has a green head, or the cow is purple? If Matisse can paint Lydia Delectorskaya's face in blue and yellow[16], then so can you.)

Like being brave, creativity is a choice you make. We can choose to foster the different elements of creativity within ourselves.

According to material compiled by Iowa State University[17], the elements of creativity can be generalised as cognitive, affective, personal, motivational, social and environmental, of which cognitive and affective are considered most important.

Cognitive elements:

- Basic knowledge (general and field-specific).
- Perceptiveness (how you *see* it).

- Originality (i.e., 'What new questions can I ask?' 'What can I invent?').

- Attraction to complexity (i.e., excitement about the problem and the different ways to solve it: 'How can I *innovate*?').

- Open-mindedness (including persistence).

- Awareness of creativity itself ('How can I approach this *creatively*?').

Affective elements include:

- Curiosity (who, what, when, where, how).

- Humour (enjoyment and playfulness).

- Risk-taking (leaning into your edge by stepping out of your comfort zone).

- Independence ('What can I do that no one else has done?' 'What would happen if I did the *opposite*?').

Creativity demonstrates itself naturally when we're doing something we love, or when we're passionate about solving a problem or overcoming a challenge. Love and passion are the key ingredients of your creative potential.

Love + passion = creative genius

When we try to squeeze ourselves into a square hole (like a job we hate), our creativity may seem to disappear. In reality it's just dormant; our creative self is bored and indifferent about the task at hand. Science supports this view: when we perform a task our prefontal cortex – also known as the 'thinking cortex' – is activated, and actually inhibits creativity. But scientists have found that being absorbed in an activity quietens the thinking cortex, so our creativity is naturally awake. If we're not harassed by task-oriented details, but rather lost in the moment of love, we can embrace our rightful capacity for original, reckless dot-connecting.

Love and passion take us beyond our thinking. Do something you love and you'll notice the attention, stillness and space the experience creates. That's what accessing your creative space feels like.

Don't get bogged down in the details of the how, get excited by the now real present moment opportunity to be a leading edge creator, to take a big enough risk to merit exponential returns.

– Jenny Sauer Klein

Identify what you love doing and your true artistic and creative potential will reveal itself. Being a leading-edge creator occurs in the moment of surrender: allow your creative experience to unfold as you do something you love. Creativity is innate. Whether you're a bike mechanic, an accountant, a dancer, or a writer, you are an artist.

What are the things that you LOVE doing? This is where you're naturally creative.

1. ....

2. ....

3. ....

4. ....

5. ....

6. ....

7. ....

8. ....

9. ....

10. ....

How does your creativity manifest while you're doing these things? List EVERYTHING – the what, where, when, why and how.

1. ....

2. ....

3. ....

4. ....

5. ....

6. ....

7. ....

8. ....

9. ....

10. ....

That's how you are creative naturally, but you can also choose to apply your creativity to things you don't love doing. The choice becomes to enjoy whatever you do by tapping into your creative gift.

What do you dislike doing?

1. ....

2. ....

3. ....

4. ....

5. ....

6. ....

7. ....

8. ....

9. ....

10. ....

How can you:

- Explore these tasks, problems or challenges from different angles?
- Enjoy the tasks, problems or challenges?
- Lean into your edge? (Step out of your comfort zone.)
- Work on the tasks, problems or challenges in a way that no one else has ever done before?

Choose to discover the depths of your creative spirit in all aspects of your life.

Complete the following sentence:

My name is .... and I am AN ARTIST!

Write the whole thing down again and again, over and over, in your own handwriting.

Then write it on five Post-its and stick them all over the house.

Discover Your Innate Talents

When you work on something that you are attracted to, your natural creativity to design, problem solve or manage can emerge regardless of whether it's what is traditionally regarded as a creative industry or not.

– Jyoti Morningstar

You are talented beyond your wildest imagination. Talent is another gift of aliveness and key to unlocking one aspect of your creative genius. Sometimes your talents are obvious because they are things you do better than any one else. Bear Grylls, British Adventurer, writer and television presenter best known for *Born Survivor* (whose TV shows have a combined audience of 1.2 billion around the globe) told John Lewis's *Edition* magazine:

I [...] found that a lot of my identity at school was being the kid that could climb the highest building and I followed that.

Follow that he did; aged 23 he became the youngest Briton ever to reach the summit of Mount Everest. His climbing talent made him unique; his inner compass directed him to follow it.

For others it's not so obvious, or so easy. Our talents can be:

1. **Forgotten.** You grew up.
2. **Weird.** Hidden from view because they're just too wacky and maybe even embarrassing.
3. **Unsustainable.** I have rent to pay. 'How could I make a living out of that?!'

Let me burst your bubble.

Steve Irwin made a living out of hunting crocodiles; he already had a passion for reptiles when, at six, he caught his first snake (a Common Brown snake). What could be more weird than a Snake Milker (extracting poison for research)? Or how about a Lipsologist (the science and art of reading lip prints)? Sustainability is organic if you bring the principles of *ahimsa* (from the section 'Be Kind' in Chapter 10) in a way that fulfils you and serves others. For example, with regard to sustainability:

1. As a yogi you might make $35 per class in your hometown, or $10,000 for a ten-person, seven-day spa-retreat in Sri Lanka.

2. If you make kick-ass BLTs (a bacon, lettuce and tomato sandwich) you could either a) work in a sandwich shop or b) create BLT.com to satisfy BLT lovers globally (hiring yourself as CEO).

3. If you have a talent for writing bite-size wisdom, you can a) annoy your friends on Facebook or b) make a career out of fortune cookie writing.

The million dollar question is: how do your talents serve you *and* others? Align what you love with the values and priorities of others and, regardless of how weird it might be, it will sustain you.

If your talents are forgotten or too weird, or your risk-taking mojo has been trampled by the status quo, it's no wonder. The trend toward homogenised education has created armies of people who've learnt the same things in the same way. It sieves our idiosyncrasies and casts them aside in favour of establishment-approved blah. If your talents aren't mainstream, you're going to need a pretty thick skin to forge ahead.

Many years ago during my school years, my boyfriend aged 16 attended a prestigious school in England, yet performed poorly against the status quo, and succeeded only in pottery. Already he was very vocal about a school system that didn't work for him and his lack of interest in following his family into insurance or ship-broking. Lucky for him he was 'cool', which gave him status and authority. Even then he was demonstrating a strong sense of leadership that was innate, regardless of grades.

The rules and restrictions of the system don't work for those who think differently (including those who are dyslexic or on the autism spectrum). As far as we have come, they are still seen as different, and expensive to cater for. On the road I've met a variety of characters who left school at 16. They are smart, savvy, interesting, creative ... they have worked and travelled, and use all the talents they've discovered along the way. They are operating raw, unfiltered and whole. They haven't been sieved.

When Alex Grant says 'Unschool yourSelf' he means 'get rid of everything that doesn't serve you'. Despite likening our school system to a kitchenware, I loved school and credit it with an awesome assortment of skills. Our sweet spot, however, lies slap bang in the middle of what can be learned and what cannot be taught. It exists where:

1. Knowledge meets imagination
2. Skills meet intuition
3. Sheer talent meets motivation

Your unique gifts and talents are concentrated, magnified and enhanced in those sweet spots.

My experience is that everyone has their own special gift and that, once discovered, acknowledged and embraced, life becomes more simple.

– Deva Premal

Your talents are innate so it is likely that you are already using them, only in a form you don't yet recognise.

How do you recognise them?

1. Ask friends, family and colleagues. Sometimes we see what you don't. It's a wood for the trees thing; our vision gets clouded by all the stories we tell ourselves, but others see the truth of it more clearly. Ask, 'What am I good at?'

2. Step out of your comfort zone. Do things you wouldn't normally do: walk a different way home; go to an event; try to meet or talk to five new people a week; try that thing (course, seminar, sport) you've talk about doing for 'x' number of years.

3. Think back to your childhood. What were you really good at as a kid?

4. What are you doing when time stops? What are you so immersed in that time figuratively stops?

5. Sometimes by accident. Who knows what skills you'll unearth in an emergency, or out of some kind of spontaneous occurrence?

Tips for discovering them:

1. Unplug. Switch off all devices and look around at the world. Without any distractions you can listen better to what's happening around you and what attracts your attention.

2. Meet new people. Embrace new connections. Our relationship dynamic is unique to each person we know, and brings out different interests and aspects of ourselves.

3. Enrol on a course. Satisfying a desire to learn that thing you always wanted to do. Enrol on an evening or online course, or do something completely random and uncharacteristic that will challenge you. What about an art or creative writing course?

4. Travel. Do something epic, life-changing and memorable. Far away from home and out of your comfort zone, I guarantee you'll discover your talents along the way.

Travel Ideas:

- **Mini:** Escape the City offer ideas for on-night Micro Adventures (http://www.microadventures.org).
- **Life-changing:** Walk the 800 km Camino de Santiago (http://www.caminoadventures.com), The Way of St James – one of the most important Christian pilgrimages for the last 1,000 years. This is the walk that fired up global icon Paulo Coelho to write *The Alchemist*.
- **Epic:** Cycle from Cairo to Cape Town over four months with Tour d'Afrique (http://tourdafrique.com).

You don't have to unplug or leave the house to ask yourself some talent-liberating questions:

What are the hard-core skills you're most proud of? Do you have a knack for algebra or Latin translation? Can you speak four languages or build a bike from scratch? Can you read an 800-page novel in three days? Can you put together a business plan in under an hour or build a website? These things are easier to quantify and articulate.

I'm most proud of:

1. ....

2. ....

3. ....

4. ....

5. ....

What are the softer skills you're most proud of? These may include character traits like compassion or empathy. They may involve other people and the way you interact with them. Can you make people feel at ease? Are you good at diffusing sticky situations? Are you calm under pressure? Do you speak in public with panache and aplomb? Can you rouse people to anger or passion just by talking? These might be less easy to quantify or articulate (but give it a go anyway).

I'm most proud of:

1. ....

2. ....

3. ....

4. ....

5. ....

What are you really, *really* good at? The most basic or most complex things. Can you complete a difficult Sudoku grid in fewer than three minutes? Can you bake exquisite walnut bread? Can you recite, word for word, every Pink Floyd track ever made? Include your senses (smell, taste, touch ...)

I am really, really good at:

1. ....

2. ....

3. ....

4. ....

5. ....

What were you really, really good at as a kid? Painting? Snakeboarding? Gymnastics? Piano? Write those down, too. As a kid I was really, really good at:

1. ....

2. ....

3. ....

4. ....

5. ....

What can you do better than anyone else you know? It can be the weirdest, funkiest, strangest thing. I don't care if it's whistling the *Star Wars* theme tune through a blade of grass, or rolling the best cigarettes in town (sure, tobacco is addictive, but rolling is an art form).

Better than anyone I know I can:

1. ....

2. ....

3. ....

4. ....

5. ....

What do others most commonly ask for your help with or advice about? Do you have knowledge or skills for which others actively seek you out?

I am the 'go-to' person for:

1. ....

2. ....

3. ....

4. ....

5. ....

What are you doing when you are completely lost in the moment? Losing time is a strong indicator that we are deeply passionate, interested, or involved in something we enjoy and are good at.

When I'm lost in the moment I am:

1. ....

2. ....

3. ....

4. ....

5. ....

What you have before you now is an extraordinary list of talent. Which ones do you make the most of? If any one thing appears in every list, it might be time to pitch your ladder against a different wall if you're not on the right one already. But first things first: start to own your talents and savour just how brilliant and unique you are.

Chapter 11: Remove the Barriers

Chapter Snapshot

- Where Do Your Core Values and Beliefs Come From?
- Assess Your Limitations
- What Are Your Judgements?
- Handle Conflict

Where Do Your Core Values and Beliefs Come From?

Which are your own true values and which do you believe because someone raised, impressed, made, forced or loved you to believe? Do you want to embody these? Do they reflect you?

– Silla Siebert

Our values identify what is important to us and our beliefs identify what we accept as truth. They determine how we think, speak and act; how we behave towards others; and how we interact with our outer world. They blend to form our attitude or our approach to life. They are visible for all to see: our actions and behaviours tell our outer world exactly what our values and beliefs are. It's therefore vital to be acutely aware of:

1. What they are.
2. Where they come from.

3. Whether they serve us.

During the course of our lives we develop a system of values and beliefs comprised of:

1. Those we are born with.
2. Those we adopt along the way, based on personal experience.
3. Those we learn from others.

Others include parents, partners, friends, teachers and the media, and present the greatest challenge to living *Absolutely on Purpose*. When we grow up or live in the shadow of someone else's values and beliefs, we may come to adopt them as our own, either automatically or as a way to avoid conflict or 'standing out'. When you align with values and beliefs that betray your own, you end up living a half life in someone else's shadow (ending up on the wrong ladder or against the wrong wall). Check in with your values and beliefs. Reflect on what is really important to you and take a look at whose truths they underpin – yours, or someone else's?

Alignment is one of Silla Siebert's core teachings. In yoga, perfect physical alignment has a synergistic effect for both the pose and your entire practice, but it's a teaching she delivers off the mat, too, emphasising the need for alignment across all the areas of your life. When you align your values and beliefs with your inner compass it results in very great synchronicity throughout all areas of your life.

One of the greatest obstacles to finding your life's task quite honestly can be your parents. We all love our parents – at least most of us do. And they mean the best. But often they're the ones that screw us up most in the sense that they want to consciously or unconsciously direct you in a path that they feel is appropriate for you.

– Robert Greene, American author

Identify the values and beliefs you adopt from others; determine whether they serve you. If they do not, transform them. They can then become powerful catalysts for your own passion, purpose and vision.

This following exercise is adapted from one I learned with Gaia.

What are three strong statements about who you are, and what is possible that you learned from:

Your mother:

....

....

....

Your father: ....

....

....

....

Your teacher (Pick one teacher, or a school): ....

....

....

....

Your ....

(insert a person, community, organisation that has been a core influence in your life, e.g. spouse, friend, lover, work, religious establishment.)

....

....

....

Reflect and re-write

1. Reflect on each one to determine whether it serves you.

2. If it doesn't serve you, cross it out.

Re-write. Flip . Search your own truth, match what's really important for you, and re-write your values and beliefs.

Make a list of your *new* core beliefs about who you are and what is possible for you. I believe ... I value...

1. ....

2. ....

3. ....

4. ....

5. ....

6. ....

7. ....

8. ....

9. ....

10. ....

Assess Your Limitations

There are no rules.

There are only limits you create with your mind

– Jenny Sauer Klein

It appears that there is one area in which we easily apply our innate creativity – in the rules we create for ourselves! These rules are limits that we create when we focus on what is missing from the inside (like knowledge and raw talent) and on the outside (like resources). If we examine our limitations more closely, we find two things:

1. They are not actually limits, but *edges*, tempting us to expand into the space they open into.
2. They are rules and restrictions that flower from the heart of the fears that we have not yet confronted, and the belief that we are not good enough.

If standing on a ledge terrifies you and unknown fears paralyse you, limitations can seem insurmountable. Get ready to shoot the usual suspects down like clay pigeons:

1. 'I don't have the money.'
2. 'I don't have the expertise.'
3. 'I don't have the time.'

I don't have the money

What is 'enough' money, and when will you ever have it? The Dreamlining Calculators and Worksheet[18] created by Tim

Ferris (author of *The 4-Hour Workweek*) demonstrates that you need less than you think. The first time I calculated the cost for the next six months it came to less than $6,000 (all essential living costs plus climbing Kilimanjaro and learning Spanish), which made me consider the full-time, swap-your-life-for-a-paycheck job a little differently....I began to wonder whether I could simply work two months a year.

Have you calculated what you actually need to get started? I'll bet it's less than you think.

If your start-up costs are still daunting, you can start smaller or smarter. You don't necessarily need:

- **To leave your job.** Not straight away! Put your evenings and weekends to good use.
- **To stay in your job.** Manifest your vision on the beach in Mexico for total living costs of $400 a month.
- **To build a website.** Instead start with a simple landing page by Launchrock (have a look at the landing page I created for the book http://signup1.absolutelyonpurpose.com) and a self-hosted wordpress blog.
- **A fancy computer.** Start with the one you've got.
- **A course.** Instead go to your local library and check out books on the subject.

List anything you think you need 'a lot' of money for. Put the $ value against it and then find a way to start 'smaller' or 'smarter'.

....

....

....

....

The fear of running out of money is like Botox: it paralyses you. Assuming you have some *moolah* right now, you're actually good to go. But you might have a vision of ending up in the gutter crying into your empty McDonald's coffee cup. I hear you. And don't be deceived; this *could* happen (the bum on the street is a real person), but *would* it? When you hit rock bottom you can move back in with your parents or stay on a friend's sofa. Your inner tribe will likely provide food and shelter because they want to see you succeed. Other options are to change your circumstances to reduce your overheads. This way you can make your money go further. Fancy a hammock in Thailand?

The experience of travel challenges your perception of money and its value. The pursuit of a location-independent lifestyle found me circling the globe, alternating travel and work. I'm frequently asked if I have a trust fund or whether I'm independently wealthy, so I think it's safe to assume that travelling is thought to be expensive. It can be, but it doesn't have to be. The truth is I'm independent, but not wealthy, because I nurture a simple lifestyle that values a rustic beach-side cabana over a Gucci handbag. Your spend reflects your values and priorities. If you have had a chance to re-write you values and priorities in the previous section, the new alignment might reveal extra funds that will buy you the additional 'head space' you need to get started, since fear is a head-centred phenomenon.

Money is simply the flow of energy which we balance by giving and receiving. When we invest in ourselves and our vision, it flows and multiplies. When we hoard it, it transforms into stagnant energy that blocks our emotional and spiritual flow. By all means keep a little aside for the proverbial rainy day, but don't keep all of it locked in your piggy bank collecting dust. It's meant to be an enabler. Use it.

I don't have the expertise

You can learn things along the way. You don't need 10,000 hours and 'phenom' status (thank you Malcolm Gladwell for the brilliant *Outliers*) to start something. You can learn what you need along the way and outsource everything else.

A wise friend told me: *You don't have to have a qualification to be qualified.* He was absolutely right. Depending on your end goal, there are other ways of developing expertise. Instead of pursuing another degree, I expended my knowledge of holistic health and beauty through freelance writing. If, like me, you have an insatiable appetite for everything, specialising in one thing for four years is counter-intuitive. I found that interviewing experts and researching for magazine features meant I could study the aspects that interested me, and I even got paid to share my discoveries with others. (Alex Grant said: 'Truth is ONE. Paths are mANY.')

Expertise in anything can be developed through dedication and focus. The internet has democratised education – there are over 700 free courses available on OpenCulture.com[19], covering everything from photography to Marxist economics. Although I was not friends with physics at school, I found myself fascinated by the Theoretical Minimum[20], a series of Standford Continuing Studies, taught by the renowned physicist Leonard Susskind.

There are also a number of independent courses that will show you the ropes in almost anything, including MBA and business skills:

1. Chris Guillebeau's Adventure Capital[21] is a twelve-month course for people with ideas or existing businesses.
2. Escape the City's MBA Start Up[22] is a three-day workshop taught by start-up experts, designed for aspiring entrepreneurs.

3. The Start-Up Training School[23] by Lea Woodward teaches you the tech and design skills you need to build your own brand and website.

4. *The Lean StartUp*[24] by Eric Ries is a step-by-step book on how to start lean and accelerate your ideas.

There are so many incredible resources out there. Want to start a spiritual community or sustainable farm? I'll bet there's someone who's written a book about it. Cue our favourite search engine: Google.

Even if you're super skilled, you'll still need to learn, adapt and re-skill along the way.

Starting lean, green and keen lies at the heart of entrepreneurship. Richard Branson unleashed his entrepreneurial zeal on *Student* magazine aged 16; twenty-seven-year-old and twenty-five-year-old Kevin Systrom and Mike Krieger founded Instagram; twenty-nine-year-old Ben Lerer founded Thrillist; twenty-nine-year-old Naveen Selvaldurai founded Foursquare. That's just the tip of the Silicon Iceberg. What lie beneath are the hundreds of other thriving initiatives, projects and organisations covering every sector possible, begun with a vivid vision of the future and often little else.

The lean, green, keen strategy

- **Lean:** Begin, armed only with a vision.
- **Green:** Learn what you need along the way.
- **Keen:** Passion and purpose are unstoppable.

The benefits of starting lean include agility, which helps build momentum fast. The benefits of being green include not knowing what isn't possible, which creates space for intuition and imagination to flourish. The benefits of being keen include the motivation to continue regardless of the challenges ahead.

I don't have the time

Just like your actions, how you spend your time reflects your highest priorities. If you're thinking or talking about a burning ambition, chances are you do have the time, but you're spending it on other activities. If reallocating your time feels like a sacrifice, then your goal is out of synch with your passion, purpose and vision.

J. K. Rowling is said to have written *The Philosopher's Stone* while her baby daughter slept. Anthony Trollope, a prolific English novelist in the Victorian era, wrote for two-and-a-half hours every morning before his job as a clerk in the British Postal Service. He wrote around forty-six novels, countless short stories, non-fiction books and plays (and our ubiquitous red letter boxes were supposedly his idea, too). How can you reallocate your time and use it to manifest a burning ambition?

I borrowed time from my social life and sleep schedule for three months when I wrote the proposal for this project. If reallocating your time feels like an investment, your passion, purpose and vision are definitely aligned.

Map out your day in 24 x 1 hour blocks, labelling each with their activity. Choose a coloured crayon and shade your fixed obligations (like work, personal trainer, family dinner, story-time with your children). Reallocate the remaining time to your burning ambition.

If the doors of perception were cleansed, everything would appear to man as it is, Infinite.

– William Blake , English poet, painter, and printmaker

There are no limits

Richie Parker is a vehicle engineer for Hendrick Motorsports. He designs chassis and body components for all four of its race teams. Born without arms, he didn't see this as a barrier to following his dreams. He designs with his feet. Watch him in action on ESPN[25].

Dergin Tokmak ('Stix') has partial paralysis in his legs after a brush with polio as a kid. This doesn't stop him from getting down on the dance floor around the world. Watch him in action on Upworthy.com[26].

What is it you tell yourself you can't do?

1. ....

2. ....

3. ....

4. ....

5. ....

6. ....

7. ....

8. ....

9. ....

10. ....

What is it that the world tells you do you that you can't do?

1. ....

2. ....

3. ....

4. ....

5. ....

6. ....

7. ....

8. ....

9. ....

10. ....

Name something that you're having trouble starting or that you've started and stopped (a project, a business or an idea). Writing a book? Starting a blog? Leaving your job? Leaving a relationship? Going back to study? Starting a business? Going freelance? Going travelling? Working from home? Exercising? Losing weight?

Idea, project, or business: ....

Then:

1. Write it down in the middle of a large piece of paper.

2. Map out the limitations ('I can't...', 'I can't because...', 'I don't have...').

3. For each, map the limitation behind it (i.e. the limitation behind the limitation).

4. Delve as deep as you can.

5. Map it to the max!

You have just deconstructed your limitation. Which limitations are you creating with your mind? Which serve you? Which don't?

Imagine these limitations didn't exist. What would be your next course of action? What would be your immediate next step with your project, business, or seed of an idea if you had the money / skills / time to do so?

Go do that thing now!

If you're 70% sure about an idea then go for it. Because if you wait till you're 100% confident in business...you'll never make a decision, you'll never get anywhere.

— Richard Reed, co-founder of Innocent Drinks

What Are Your Judgments?

If you could live your life without fear, worry about what 'others' will say, or your own mind saying no, what would you do?

Go do that right now.

– Hemalayaa

What we think about ourselves — and what we think others think about us — influences our actions and behaviours. While a limitation is like a rule or circumstance, a judgement is more like an opinion. Like being brave or creative, we can choose to judge ourselves with love, kindness and truth.

Are there things you do or don't do because of what you think about yourself, or because of what others think about you?

Mini self-judgement quiz

You have a volcano-sized pimple on your chin. Do you:

1. Ignore it and get on with your business?
2. Squeeze it till it bleeds, apply cover-up like Plaster of Paris, and cancel your date?
3. Stay home until it disappears?

You're at a party where you know nobody and you're favourite track comes on. Do you:

1. Dance with wild abandon because you just love this tune?
2. Down a few drinks and then get down on the dance floor?
3. Watch on the side-lines while others strut their stuff?

You're dream job is advertised. Do you:

1. Apply immediately, because you're the best person for the job?
2. Procrastinate, because you need to update your CV?
3. Don't apply, because you're not qualified?

Jokes and hypothetical questions aside, and truth be told, you are beautiful, regardless of the pimple; you are most sexy and alluring when you're dancing with wild abandon; and you're more than qualified to determine the direction and speed of your career trajectory.

What we think about ourselves either holds us back or propels us forward. When you own your amazingness, you project it like a shining orb and everyone will see it. All *we* see is what you *own*.

I judge myself when I'm comparing myself to someone. When people dazzle us it can be momentarily blinding, until we remember that those sparkly bits are reflections of ourselves. We just happen to see them in others. I love people who are smart, passionate, purposeful and visionary, and have learned to identify these qualities in myself. I can feel inspired by the people I admire without feeling disempowered or 'less than'.

When you connect with your true nature and accept who you are without judging yourself, you are yourself, completely.

– Lawrence Quirk

We play many roles in our lives, but underneath them all is the *satya* of it – the absolute, unchangeable truth of who we are. If you can own your amazingness you give yourself permission to be the most raw, unapologetic version of You, all of the time.

Liberate your Self from all judgement and dazzle us with your amazingness.

In what ways do you judge yourself, and what does this inhibit you from doing? You can reframe this question by identifying what you don't do, and why.

1. ....

2. ....

3. ....

4. ....

5. ....

6. ....

7. ....

8. ....

9. ....

10. ....

In what ways do others judge you, and what does this inhibit you from doing?

Think of the things that people tell you that you can't do and why. Think of the things that people have said – either in jest, or during some form of conflict – that have affected what you think you can and cannot do.

1. ....

2. ....

3. ....

4. ....

5. ....

6. ....

7. ....

8. ....

9. ....

10. ....

What qualities in other people do you compare yourself against?

1. ....

2. ....

3. ....

4. ....

5. ....

6. ....

7. ....

8. ....

9. ....

10. ....

In what forms do you embody these same qualities? Think think think! And then think more until this is really clear for you.

1. ....

2. ....

3. ....

4. ....

5. ....

6. ....

7. ....

8. ....

9. ....

10. ....

What qualities do you wish you embodied?

1. ....

2. ....

3. ....

4. ....

5. ....

6. ....

7. ....

8. ....

9. ....

10. ....

Where do you embody these *wish list* qualities? What form are they in? (Don't move on from this question until you've come up with at least five.)

1. ....

2. ....

3. ....

4. ....

5. ....

6. ....

7. ....

8. ....

9. ....

10. ....

Handle Conflict

If you are at war with your family, your friends or your children, then you are at war with your Self.

– Anne-Marie Newland

Conflict is an energy vampire. Whatever form conflict takes, when you handle it, it frees up space.

It takes two to tango

Some people unleash your inner Hulk, or just rub you up the wrong way. Newsflash: It's the dynamic between the two of you that is causing the conflict. Its shape and form feeds off your attitude towards it. When you take responsibility for the role you play in its creation and then *handle it*, either by letting it go or confronting it, you create space.

Based on the consensus of everyone I've ever met, I'm contrary, stubborn and opinionated which, according to their tone, are not good traits. I'm no stranger to conflict, but it has become the cherry on the icing on my cake of self-awareness because it presents opportunities to get to know myself better. I have spent the last three years reconciling myself to knowing that conflict is the best cherry life can offer you (and I don't even like glacé cherries). By confronting conflict we come face to face with ourselves.

When you develop a method of handling conflict, you can tap into the truth and wisdom it harbours. Whatever the trigger, it prods your beliefs and values, and provokes a cross-check.

When your ego is ready to step back from being right, you can make a solid decision about whether to let it go or go deeper, where you learn more. You can also identify whether you need help (phone a friend?) or more time to deconstruct it.

What does conflict reflect back to you?

Just as the qualities we admire in others reflect our own, so too does the cross-fire of conflict. Our beliefs, values, limitations and judgements are provoked into battle, armed and ready to win. However, if we wage war only to be right, the winning won't be the end of it. If no lesson is learned we will face the same conflict on a different field with a different army, time and time again. This is a red flag for self-examination: 'Why do I repeatedly attract the same types of conflict?'

Should you let it go?

If you're waging war because you need to be right, scold your ego and step down. Use your energy for worthwhile battles that encourage you to explore the depths of your Self.

If you're afraid to confront the issue, it might be worthwhile examining your fears before you surrender. Head back to the section 'Be Brave' in Chapter 10 for a thorough analysis of your fear. It could be that the wisdom you gain from going deeper is worth the confrontation required.

Should you go deeper?

When your intuition tells you there is more at stake than winning, go deeper:

Put yourself in their shoes. What is their point of view? Can you see where they are coming from? Do they simply need to be heard or given permission to express themselves?

Face to face, acknowledge their point of view. Once you validate their point of view, their attention is yours. It's now your turn to speak, using the principles of kindness (*ahimsa*) and truthfulness (*satya*). Where once there may have been cross-fire there is now a mutually desired cease-fire, and the space to communicate and learn.

Three things useful to keep in mind when troubleshooting conflict:

1. What is it reflecting back to me?
2. Do I need to be 'right'?
3. How can I validate their point of view?

Four steps to conflict resolution

1. **Identify a conflict.** If you can't think of an obvious conflict, do a quick mental scan through your family, friends, colleagues and acquaintances and stop when you feel your stomach turn. This is your conflict (unless you're in love with them, in which case a stomach flip is normal).

   ....

2. **What is this conflict reflecting back to you?** Describe your thoughts and feelings about the other person(s) involved.

   ....

   ....

   ....

   ....

   ....

3. Do I just need to be 'right'?

- If YES, let it go.
- IF NO, are you afraid to go deeper? IF NO, let it go. If YES, run through the chapter 'Be Brave' and then go deeper.

4. Go Deeper.

- Put yourself in their shoes. What do they think, feel or want? What are they saying? Why?

- Validate their point of view face to face. Explain your point of view with kindness and truthfulness. Create space. Communicate.

- What have you learned about yourself?

- What have you learned about your opponent? They might now be one of your greatest teachers.

How to identify recurring conflicts

What types of conflict do you encounter frequently? Think of your family, relationships, friendships and work (in fact any area of your life).

Recurring conflict: ....

- What areas of life does the conflict invade?
- Who are the sparring partner(s)?
- What values, beliefs, limitations and judgements do they challenge?
- What does this reflect back to you?
- What is the opportunity?
- What can you learn?

Chapter 12: Practical Strategies to Get Started

Chapter Snapshot:

- New Plan: Plan 'F'
- Define Your Own Metrics for Success
- Connect with Your Tribe
- Find Your Teacher
- Dedication and Focus
- Start at the End
- Let Go

New Plan: Plan 'F'

Following your passion requires a willingness to go against social trends and expectations.

– Ted Grand

Fuck expectations and social trends. Fuck the naysayers and people who tell you that you can't or shouldn't. Fuck the people who tell you what to do. Fuck the attitudes of parents, siblings, friends, even if they're trying to protect you. Fuck the kids at school who bullied or teased you. Fuck the teachers who told you that you wouldn't amount to anything, or who told you to colour within the lines. Fuck the preachers and leaders who told you what was right and what was wrong. Fuck the establishments that dictate the status quo. Fuck the opinions of others. Fuck the judgments and limitations you place on yourself. Fuck the fear of no money. Fuck the fear of failing. Fuck the fears that paralyse you. Fuck the fear of fear itself. Fuck the risks. Fuck your weaknesses. Fuck the beliefs and values that hold you back. Bring your ideas to life and say: 'Fuck it' to anyone or anything that sits between you and your dream. BE your own rebellion.

Am I advocating non-conformity for the sake of it? No. Be yourself. Be deliberate. Create your own meaning. The trouble with non-conformity 'for the sake of it' is that you end up non-conforming, just like everyone else. Like the rebellious teenager who gets a tattoo to defy their parents. When we do things to spite others, or for the sake of being non-conformist, we're simply perpetuating conformity.

Overthrow existing beliefs and structures by creating your own. Be anti-establishment because you've found a better way. Be non-conformist because you can't be any other way. Confront challenges with solutions. Confront problems with panache and excitement. Be yourself, and you have a natural act of rebellion right there. Demonstrate your values and you'll have your first follower. Be consistent and eventually you'll have your tribe. Be who you are and you'll attract the people you need to bring your vision to life. Be passionate. Be steeped in purpose. You don't have to be non-conformist for the sake of it. You just have to be You.

What social trends and expectations make your blood boil?

1. ....

2. ....

3. ....

4. ....

5. ....

6. ....

7. ....

8. ....

9. ....

10. ....

How do you rebel against them?

1. ....

2. ....

3. ....

4. ....

5. ....

6. ....

7. ....

8. ....

9. ....

10. ....

Who and what can you say *fuck it* to?

1. ....

2. ....

3. ....

4. ....

5. ....

6. ....

7. ....

8. ....

9. ....

10. ....

Define Your Own Metrics for Success

This is a world where everything is on loan to us. We lose it all. Our wealth, our property, our family, our material beauty. Our control of our own life is painfully limited. Yes the material path is a sucker's bet. We all lose. What we are qualified to do is to give, to serve, to love.

– Raghunath

Materialism is not a twentieth-century construct. Humans have loved beautiful, luxurious things that had no utility for thousands of years. Pharaohs were buried in tombs filled with luxury objects: spices, culinary delicacies, gold and jewellery (and their own live slaves, but that's another matter).

Stuff is not a bad thing. We surround ourselves with things that make us happy: clothes, books, perfumes, and so on. But stuff has a dark side: materialism takes on a sinister edge when we prioritise it over emotional, intellectual, spiritual and cultural values.

Stuff can be very dense in that it can take up space, both in terms of physical space and mental, emotional and spiritual space. When we desire more stuff it detracts us from our *dharma*, our spiritual path, and when it overflows it can overwhelm us (when we hoard), and perhaps induce fear (someone might take it from us).

In truth, we cannot measure our success against stuff alone. You might be sitting in the Jacuzzi at your hillside mansion that houses all the stuff you ever wanted, yet still have an aching void within. Is that success? You might even continue to fill that void with stuff, but if you were to define your metrics for success beyond the material, and explore the spectrum that guides you through to your spiritual calling, you could bask in your jacuzzi blissed-out and fulfilled. When metrics for success including connecting and collaborating with others and the planet, you fill the spiritual void by co-creating a better world. You may then appreciate stuff differently, or find you need less of it.

> *There's no point doing something that doesn't interest you for an abstract goal like money or fame, because, even if you have some success in doing that thing, it still won't bring you satisfaction.*
>
> – Jyoti Morningstar

Metrics for success are unique to you

Don't be judged by someone else's idea of success. Everything you do has an unlimited metric spectrum, from just showing up and getting started, through to revolutionising the way we live. They can range from personal to global (or, if you're like Richard Branson, galactic). They can be physical, emotional, mental, spiritual, or any combination of those. The success for your career, project or business can be measured against how you feel and the impact that it has on others. Take this book, for example. It's a success because I'm writing it; because it's my *truth* and my gift to you, and it's a vision in line with my passions and purpose. My success metrics are:

1. Write it. (Tick.)

2. Publish it. (Tick.)

3. Create a transformational shift in the life and perspective of just one person (Tick).

4. Achieve best-seller status.

5. Sell 100,000 copies.

6. Inspire an entire generation of people to live *Absolutely on Purpose*.

7. Spark a movement that ignites the search for passion, purpose and vision.

8. Contribute to sustainable social change for the recipient organisations of the *Absolutely on Purpose* fund.

9. Create a multimedia toolkit to expand the key messages of the book.

10. Invitation to appear on *Super Soul Sunday* with Oprah and *Q&A Tuesday* with Marie Forleo, and to interview with my other mentors.

(And that's just ONE project.)

Develop your own success metrics

Knowing what we want to feel, and what we'd like others to feel, do, think or have, is a great way to measure our success. Knowing on what level we want to effect change can help us to create a checklist for what we choose to put our energy into.

For this exercise you can focus on yourself, your career, or any project, business, or goal you have in the works. You can go through it several times for different projects or goals.

My focus for this exercise: ....

How do you want to feel:

- Physically:
- Mentally:
- Emotionally:

- Spiritually:

As a result of the focus you have chosen, what would you like others to:

- Feel:
- Think or believe:
- Do:
- Have:

On what level do you want to effect change? What kind of change(s) do you want to effect at this / these level(s)?

- Personal or family:
- Local or community:
- National:
- Global:
- Galactic:

Write down your top five metrics for success. Based on you answers above:

1. ....

2. ....

3. ....

4. ....

5. ....

Connect with Your Tribe

Ask for help. You cannot solve some problems alone.

– Silla Siebert

Building relationships and having conversations with people who share our values and beliefs can motivate us when facing the daunting task of starting up.

When you change tack it's easy to feel alone. But you're not. Or at least you don't have to be.

Finding and connecting with your tribe is a game-changer. Interacting with like-minded souls helps you feel understood, supported and safe; a delicious safety net when you're exploring uncharted territory. It's possible to find a groundswell of support in people you have never met before; in contrast, (and worst case) zero support amongst friends and family. Embrace the new world order. Get tribal.

We are meant to collaborate and awaken alongside each other in a wide horizontal embrace.

– Sianna Sherman

We have a yearning to feel part of something larger than ourselves, connect with others, and return to the community paradigm. Digital communities have revealed the thirst for community life long forgotten in the cluttered urban jungle, and through them we're seeing a resurgence in the desire to connect in real time. Many social networks have regular real-time gatherings to build and nurture real relationships with real people – InterNations, Levo League and Project Eve, to name a few (I've already mentioned Escape the City). Some also offer courses, seminars and webinars that teach new skills and refine existing ones, transforming theory into practice. They offer problem-solving, guidance and advice, mentoring and help and support in many forms, and across many areas.

Reach out to someone safe who is on your wavelength. Talk to them about your ideas just to hear what you have to say. Talking aloud uses a different brain pathway where new insights come through. AVOID sharing your stuff with people who don't get you.

— Jill Badonsky, author of *The Muse is In: An Owner's Manual to Your Creativity*

How do you find your tribe? Be truthful about who you are and what you believe in. Follow your passions and the bread-crumbs will lead you to your tribe(s). Put all your cards on the table. Tell people what you're doing and what you're looking for. Respond to random invites to random, related or relevant events. Seize opportunities to meet new people and do new things. Tell your story everywhere you go, and you'll find that you're building the relationships and having the conversations that will support your vision. Put yourself out there, and it will happen effortlessly.

How to connect with your tribe

1. Be vocal. Tell your story everywhere you go. Your tribe will naturally be drawn to you.

2. Explore social networks in your areas of interest that have real world meet-ups. Talking to real people with similar dreams and goals, face to face, is inspiring. Chatting with someone over a G&T takes the pressure off and creates and inspires perspective shifts during the most challeng-ing times.

3. Put a listing on Craigslist Meetup Groups. Doesn't matter how weird or wacky. They have everything on here.

4. Follow people like you in your location. Twitter and Face-book are the obvious platforms. Initiate dialogue with them: ask questions; respond with answers; arrange cof-

fee dates. You can connect with anyone, from other female entrepreneurs to green fingers with urban gardens.

5. Tell everyone you know about what you're doing, and ask for introductions. People know people – including your friends, family and colleagues – and personal introductions through trusted contacts are a great way to meet like-minded people. Tell your story to everyone you know, and you're bound to hear: 'I know someone who...' And, likewise, you can ask: 'Who do you know who I could be talking to?'

6. Follow up magazine, blog, and media leads. Send emails, ask questions, attend events and talk to the people doing, writing and talking about what you're doing. It's a great way to create a network of experts and build your own credibility. They might even be interested in coffee or mentoring you.

7. Enjoy the clean slate. Starting from scratch means you can attract all the people who affirm to a higher good, and will be most supportive and impactful towards your vision. It will also inspire reciprocation; when you want to be part of something, you are more generous with your own ideas and help others. Collaborate and you magnify the impact of your tribal experience.

8. Check in with yourself regularly. Am I being true to myself? Am I telling my own story? This will ensure that the connections you make are the right ones. You'll attract the perfect tribe.

Find Your Teacher

Search for your teacher and invest your time in what is taught. Not only will it help you get where you want to go, but on your journey of discovery you will nourish the world in the process.

– Jonathan Monks

Remember the teachers who shared so much passion and enthusiasm with you that there was no doubt, even then, that they loved teaching, just as much as you loved being taught? The committed and fluid master-disciple relationship that characterises knowledge sharing in ancient cultures is still alive, though it's not the norm.

Instead of a two-way flow, our education system is for the most part characterised by a far less intimate dissemination of information and knowledge rather than the cultivation of wisdom. The system is built around test scores, which we can access simply by drawing on our short-term memory, rather than engaging our own thinking and ideas. (Imagine a nation of powerful, independent thinkers ...)

In the ancient tradition, the disciple commits to not only learning but also to assisting the master in the development of his knowledge. Likewise the master commits to maintaining and improving his skills and knowledge throughout ongoing training with the disciple. It's an exquisite two-way flow – each person is enriched.

I was lucky to experience this. Latin was the only subject at school I truly loved. My teachers were passionate storytellers and inspired historians. They must have been through Virgil's *Aeneid* a zillion times, but with each passage read – completely lost in the dizzying fever of translation, and like the most inspired artists – it was as if they were translating the story for the first time. It seems that true masters relish a lifetime of learning, and they share their knowledge in two ways:

• Following original texts and teachings to the letter – this is pretty much recording and memorising, then passing it on.

- *Practising lineage* – mastering, realising, understanding, and developing knowledge before passing it on to the next generation, for them to do the same.

The latter method is the heart of invention and creativity; it's a very awesome way of blending the knowledge you've curated together with your own unique ideas. You can blend your wisdom with your idea of the future to innovate. Remember:

Wisdom + An Idea of the Future = Vision.

Having a relationship with someone who has gone before us takes away the pressure of having to create immediate change by ourselves.

– Kate Ellis

Like connecting with your tribe, finding your teacher(s) takes the heat of getting from A to B by yourself. The relationship gives you permission to be truthful about where you are right here right now, slow down, create space, and gather momentum towards your goal in your own time.

Teachers have perfect timing. They appear when you are ready for them. I was contemplating a return to the corporate world out of sheer 'brokeness' and gloom when I walked into Chris Calarco's yoga class in Portland, Oregon. With a few well-chosen words between postures, he reminded me that no matter how hard things get, we always come unstuck. He said that by leaning into our edge – expanding – we can reconnect to our flow while maintaining full view of our vision. That was my first class with Chris, and he immediately became my teacher.

How to find your teacher

Teachers can be obvious (i.e. qualified), or experienced in the area you want to pursue (i.e. a mentor). They can deliver wisdom that lasts a lifetime in a five-minute window, or throughout the course of your life. Some people are natural teachers, like a delivery vehicle for universal wisdom. In short, teachers come in many shapes and forms. Ancient wisdom goes that when you are ready for your teacher they appear as if by *abracadabra* (Aramaic for 'I create as I speak'). Be open to teaching and wisdom from any source, and the teacher or the teaching will arrive 'on time'.

How do you know if a teacher is right for you?

The checklist:

1. **What attracts you to this teacher?** Does your connection with them serve and support you? *Awe* is disempowering. *Inspiration* is empowering. Check that it is an empowering connection that fires you up.

2. **Do they serve you and your highest good?** Do they have an authentic intention to share their knowledge with you, or are they committed to boosting their ego? Are they committed to helping you achieve your highest potential, even if it were to go way beyond their own?

3. **Who are their teachers?** Do they have a good and continuing relationship with their own teachers? Are they committed to ongoing learning and training?

4. **What are their other students like?** Would you like to be like them? Do they resonate with you? Do they seem empowered? Do they embody what you are looking for?

5. **Do they practice what they preach?** Is their lifestyle at odds with what they teach you? (Do they advocate a vegetarian lifestyle and then go home for a bacon sandwich?) They don't have to be purist, but their actions should be congruent with their teachings. The best teachers share their own challenges with us.

6. **Are they committed to continuous study and self-improvement?** Someone committed to their own personal development will also be committed to inspiring yours.

7. **Is there a two-way flow?** If this is a face-to-face relationship? Does it feel mutually beneficial? Is their teaching experience part of their own learning curve? Are they open to learning from you, too?

When to move on from a teacher

Equally important as finding your teacher is knowing when to move on. This needn't be as dramatic as severing ties completely, but when the time is right, letting go creates space for new teachers to appear.

Each time I practice a new yoga style with a different teacher, my understanding expands exponentially. Richard taught me breath. Gaia taught me space. Raphan taught me strength. Silla taught me alignment (and some kick-ass body sculpt). And that's just during one year. Through all my teachers I have a self-practice that is spacious and strong, grounded in alignment and anchored by my breath. The best strategy for any aspect of life, art and entrepreneurship is pic'n'mix. Mix up your inspiration, teaching and learning for exponential growth.

Variety is the spice of life. Maybe it's time to get a new coach or mentor, or simply unsubscribe from a newsletter. When I feel like I've learned enough from a visionary entrepreneur, I unsubscribe to create space in my inbox. Creating space – everywhere possible – remains the single most important teaching of my life.

Acknowledging your lineage is a powerful gesture towards the master-disciple relationship. Raphan Kebe invites his teachers to participate in his teacher-training programme. 'I loved meeting and practising with his teachers and seeing how their practice might have impacted his,' says Thaïs Mayne Hanvey, one of Raphan's teacher-training students. Demonstrating the role your teachers play in the evolution of your own art form is a wonderful way to pay tribute to the master-disciple relationship.

It doesn't matter if everything has been done before. By adding your own creative spark, energy and ideas to something that already exists, you're creating a brand new interpretation AND experience of what has gone before it. That's innovation. There is no limit where there is endless possibility.

Everything that can be invented – has already been invented.

– Charles Duell, Commissioner of the United States Patent Office, 1899

The jury is out on whether Charles was misquoted.

Dedication and Focus

Following your passion is to me being able to equally enjoy and put up with, let's be honest here, the amount of work required to reach your goal.

– Raphan Kebe

Cue: Yoda, one of the most wise fictional characters ever. (Do. Or Not Do. There is No Try.)

Dedication (D) and focus (F) are tethered to your passion, purpose and vision. You might need to bring in the big gun (discipline) occasionally, but D&F arrive uninvited when you're doing what you love. About those times you said, 'I wish I played the guitar', 'I wish I spoke Spanish', 'I wish I worked for myself'. It's D&F that separates the dreamers from the achievers. Our D&F reflect our highest priorities.

No matter what your passion, if you stand confident in what you have to offer, pursue it with diligence, and work in integrity, I believe it's impossible not to succeed.

– Ashley Gayle Stuhr

D&F assessment

Creating a plan is the first step. You've put pen to paper (or fingertips to keyboard) and you've outlined first steps. As that list grows, the requirements of the project (literally, physically, mentally, emotionally and practically) start to dawn on you. At this point you either forge ahead with D&F or go to the pub for a G&T.

Even with a rough plan, your D&F will be challenged along the way. I spent three months working on a book proposal (a bit like a business plan for a book) and thought I knew what was in store for me. Boy was I deluded! Nothing could have prepared me for the sheer amount of D&F required to complete the project. However, my talent surfaced, my passion and purpose held true, my vision held strong, and my D&F pulled me through.

Are you prepared to do what it takes?

What are some of the things you have said that you wish you did? What stopped you from following through?

1. ....

2. ....

3. ....

4. ....

5. ....

List any ideas, projects or businesses that you have not yet started, or have not followed through with. State the single most important factor that prevented you from doing so.

1. ....

2. ....

3. ....

4. ....

5. ....

Do you notice any recurring themes above? Other people? Finances? Timing? Lack of experience? Fear? Lack of genuine passion?

Start at the End

I sometimes start my self-practice, and even my classes, with the end.

– Raphan Kebe

Reverse engineering is an art and science. The term describes the process of taking something apart to see its component parts. Used by software engineers, life coaches and marketers, it's a great way to determine what's required so that you can set goals to propel you from A (where you are now) to exciting point B (where your vision manifests). By dissecting your vision into its key elements, you can more easily identify the steps you need to take to manifest it.

Think of it as working backwards. Take a mountain bike for instance. If you take it apart piece by piece and see all the component parts on the floor, you'll know exactly what's required in putting it together again (perhaps even a formula or strategy emerges). Focusing on your end game – vision – and understanding the requirements to get you there, will help you do four things:

1. See exactly what's involved in manifesting your vision.

2. Make an informed assessment about whether you have the D&F to navigate the immediate, mid-term and long-term goals.

3. Pay attention to what your heart says (how it feels).

4. Help you chart the path to your destination.

Your plan does not have to be detailed at the start, only your vision needs to be vivid because this is the destination. Plans are just a spring board for action to get you on the path. They adapt and flow with you and your vision, responding to decisions and directions you take along the way. Starting at the end – with a clear, vivid vision – can kick-start your beginning.

Questions for starting at the end

Project yourself five years into the future (inspired by the classic 'What is your five year plan' question). It's 2018 and your vision has manifested. What have you achieved and how do you describe it to other people? Where are you? How do you feel? What does it look like? What impact has it had? What are the different aspects of its contribution?

1. **How did you achieve it?** What were the key steps involved in achieving your vision? How did you get from A to B?

2. **How did you decide which path to take?** What factors were involved? What determined your decisions?

3. **What advice would you give to others just starting out?** How would you inspire them to set their own goals to achieve their vision?

4. **Get back into present time. Take your vision apart.** What are the component parts or elements required to achieve it?

Let Go

If you have a soul-deep impulse for change, ASK for it.

BELIEVE in your heart that you are capable, deserving and trustworthy of this gift.

And then just sit back and RECEIVE.

– Erica Jago

Our *no pain, no gain* culture short-circuits our ability to let go as we drive ourselves faster and harder towards achieving our goals. You might want to consider switching gears. When we put the pedal to the metal, we deny ourselves the absolute pleasure of watching our vision unfold. We don't have to toil away to the last moment to see our dreams come to fruition. Ease your foot off the accelerator and enjoy the ride. You've set the ball in motion. Through your intention, dedication and focus you have *asked*. It's time to *believe* and *receive*.

In my early media days I would resign without a job to go to, believing that if I created a space another job would appear as if by *abracadabra*. Sometimes I didn't even have the time to update my CV; I'd receive a phone call from a recruiter or a tip on a great opportunity and, boom!, another role. While you're reading this book I'll be working on my next project, having set this one free to be whatever it can be. There's only so much you can do to create success. Not to get too hippy on you, but there comes a point when you have to step away and set it free to allow all the effort you've put in create its own momentum. This, in effect, will tell you the next steps. (If it has a life of its own, you're on to a winner!).

You are a divine receiver and transmitter, and to follow your path, through the moments of fear and doubt and exhaustion, are to allow your true destiny to unfold in the most perfect and organic of ways.

– Jenny Sauer Klein

This strategy is especially effective when you feel stuck. I love the movie analogy here: If your life was a movie, how would it unfold? Would it be a fast-paced action-adventure, or a slow drama in four acts? A great screenwriter knows not to create too much back story so the scenes don't drag. They ensure this by adhering to the present so the characters can inhabit the moment and draw us into the story. How much back story does your movie have? Is your movie (life, project, idea, business, relationship) dragging? Can you cut the back story and give the scenes a bit of space; the characters a bit of air?

Gaia reminded us that this is a one-time limited-edition experience – you get to watch this movie only once. At some point we have to let go and enjoy the fruit of our intentions and efforts, and allow the plot to develop organically (without our constant re-writes) and let the other characters ad lib a little. Free yourself from the mental bondage that squeezes the life-giving breath out of the story of your life. It's like making a good espresso: you gotta let it percolate.

Take a deep breath. Let it go. Trust.

Loosen your grip = freedom + space

How can you surrender? If you're the party planner, let someone else do it; resist the urge to perfect your kids homework (they have it covered); try something extreme like a skydive or bungee jump; let someone else decide what you're wearing for the day. Think of the areas where you have to be in control and flip them to discover how to surrender.

1. ....

2. ....

3. ....

4. ....

5. ....

6. ....

7. ....

8. ....

9. ....

10. ....

What's going on in your life right now that you *could* let go of? You might feel stuck over a project, situation, relationship, visa application... What's pushing your control-freak button?

1. ....

2. ....

3. ....

4. ....

5. ....

6. ....

7. ....

8. ....

9. ....

10. ....

Then ask yourself these questions:

- What are you really *asking* for in this situation?
- Do you *believe* it is for the highest good?
- Can you allow yourself to *receive* your intended outcome?

Ask. Believe. Receive.

Chapter 13: The Slate Is Clean

Your slate is clean. Whatever you discovered, you're primed to magnify your potential in any area of life, art, and entrepreneurship. You can be masterful in all these areas simply by showing up as the most raw and authentic version of yourself.

As you become more conscious of your thoughts and actions, and feel what your heart and body are telling you, you allow for the perfect experience to unfold as far as the universe is infinite. As you breathe, move, find your stillness, cultivate space and connect with nature you fortify yourself from the inside out, handling the outside world with grace and panache. As you learn to be kind and truthful, your mask drops and you can forge stronger connections with others. As you confront fear and other weaknesses you discover hidden strength. As you claim creativity and talent as your birthright, you unleash your creative genius. As you align your own values, confront your limitations and judgements and handle conflict you begin to thrive. As you say *fuck it* to everything that gets in your way and define your own metrics for yourself, you are giving permission to others to do so too. As you connect with your tribe and find your teacher, you take comfort in community and collaboration. As you choose the path of dedication and focus, and reverse-engineer your vision, you come to understand that you have what it takes. As you let go you continue to allow the perfect experience to unfold. Your slate is clean.

Brainstorming Your Passion, Purpose and Vision

Are you ready to brainstorm your passions, purpose and vision? You may have a crystal clear idea of what they may be, or perhaps no idea at all. Regardless, these questions frame a new lens to create and express them, and so you might have a few surprises in store.

Brainstorms are great, because there is no right or wrong answer; nothing is edited or censored, even your thoughts. They are a platform for creativity and play, so be brave and allow the voice of your deep self to speak.

How to Use This Section

After you've completed 'Clean Your Slate', work through the Passion, Purpose and Vision questions in order. Complete it in one sitting, or over three evenings.

What You'll Need

Post-its and a pen.

How to Approach the Questions

1. Take a deep breath and feel into each question. Reflect on the questions for as long as you like. Take your time. Be still. Create space. Breathe. Move. Connect with nature. Write a *haiku*. Whatever it is that encourages your deep self to speak, do that. If you get stuck, take a break and come back. (Be still. Create space. Breathe. Move. Connect with nature. Write a *haiku*.)

2. Write. One idea or answer per Post-it.

3. Write and keep writing.

4. Write down everything. This section is about articulating and expressing your passion, purpose and vision, maybe for the first time. The weirder and wackier the better. Listen out for the voice of your deep self to speak. Write

down what it says. The only rule: no editing or censorship
– let it flow!

Chapter 14: Express Your Passion

Power to the passionate – the weirder and wackier the better.

– Jessica Robertson

Passion Questions

1. How do you spend your:

    - **Time.** What do you do with your time? Look at your twenty-four hours.

    - **Money.** What do you spend your money on? Be specific – i.e. crime novels, cycling gear, Gucci handbags.

    - **Energy.** What makes you feel energised? (Or what do you do when you have the most energy?)

2. **If money were no object, what would you be doing with your day / week / life?** There is no rent to pay, no bills to worry about and no food to buy. What would you do instead? These could be the dream jobs, childhood dreams, back burner dreams, rainy day ideas, the things you say you would do if you didn't need money.

3. **What is the single focus and activity that would keep you absolutely fascinated and motivated for the rest of your life?** Remember: Steve Irwin hunted crocodiles, and you can get paid to analyse lip imprints. What would keep you fascinated?

4. **What does your stuff say about you?** The story of who we are is told through the things (yes! the stuff) we surround ourselves by – the objects, the labels, the brands. Look at the things in your personal space, starting with the objects

x

(e.g. books), the type of objects (e.g. the genre), and then the brands. Do this with all your everyday objects: clothes, electronics, kitchen equipment, furniture, and skincare products. They tell a detailed story about your passions and what's important to you. Look at them and see what they say. Over time we collect things that have meaning for us.

5. **Think of the activities you love to do.** Why do you do them? What is your underlying motivation?

6. **What is the happiest hour of your day or week?** Which hour do you look forward to the most and why? What are you doing, thinking and saying in this hour?

7. **What do you shift your normal sleeping pattern for?** We all love to sleep. What gets you up outside of your normal sleep-wake cycle without complaint? (I need eight hours sleep, but when I have to catch a flight, two will do!)

8. **What do you talk about most often?** What do you bring into all your conversations, regardless of who they're with? This is one to ask your friends; you might be surprised by what they come back with.

9. **What drives you completely mad as a hatter?** As you go about your day-to-day activities, what makes you f-'n'-blind, boils your blood, makes you want to punch your fist through a window, drives you bonkers?

10. **What breaks your heart?** When you're out and about and look at the world around you; when you're in deep conversation with your friends about the world and how it works; when you read media updates and ponder our climate, what makes your heart ache?

11. **If you had two hours extra a day, what would you do with them?** What single activity would you do? (Mentioning sleep is not helpful, unless you would like to be a research subject for REM activity.)

12. **If you had one extra day in the week, how would you spend it?** Map out a day from 6 a.m. to 10 p.m.

13. **What are you curious about?** What do you daydream about when you're bored? What questions frequently pop into you head? What questions do you ask others? What do you wonder about? Where does your mind drift off to in spare moments?

14. **What did your parents consistently tell you not to do?** You may have stopped doing something you loved because it didn't fit into their idea of *normal* or *good*.

Next steps:

Organise the Post-its into themes. Your answers will form natural groups. What themes have emerged? They might be nouns (shoes, compassion or children), activities (yoga, kite-surfing or travelling), verbs (listening, fixing or advising) . How you theme your passion(s) is up to you.

1. ....

2. ....

3. ....

4. ....

5. ....

6. ....

7. ....

8. ....

9. ....

10. ....

What are the umbrella themes? Do any of the themes connect and overlap? You may find that some or all sit happily under an umbrella theme.

1. ....

2. ....

3. ....

4. ....

5. ....

Can you articulate passion in a sentence? Or is it more like a list?

My passion is:

....

....

Chapter 15: Express Your Purpose

Your life purpose is always there. However, it takes the time and space to observe your own thoughts and figure out what it is that you're manifesting.

– Lawrence Quirk

Purpose Questions

1. **What do people consistently come to you for help and advice with?** These moments highlight your most natural sense of purpose. Consider what they ask, how you help, and why they ask you.

2. **What is / are the thread(s) that unite(s) all the major and minor roles you've played so far?** Even if the jobs are seemingly worlds apart, like your job as a barista at university or college, and your current position as an architect, what are the common denominators? Again, consider the what, the how, and the why. There will be a how or a why that connects all the dots, because how we do one thing is how we do everything. List all your roles and think about the thread that connects them (think of people, skills, environment, etc.).

3. **What moments, projects, hobbies, people, organisations, or businesses inspire you?** The things that inspire us reconnect us to our purpose. When or where are you bathed in absolute inspiration? What are you doing in these moments? Where are you? Who are you with? Why are you doing it?

4. **What information, knowledge, or skills do you crave or thirst for?** Our deepest longings might reveal how we could best be of service. After all, and in my case, the best way to become an expert in a subject is to write a book about it.

5. **What major challenges, transformations and events have characterised your life so far?** How did you handle, heal, transform, or live with them? Insights captured through personal experience can reveal a unique perspective or approach that points you to your purpose. They can be physical, mental, emotional or spiritual. Chances are there are others who would benefit from hearing what you have to say about it.

6. **What sphere of life most intrigues you?** Are you most interested in your own personal development? Do you find yourself more interested in what's happening at home or your local neighbourhood? Are you more interested in what's happening at a national level? Is it at a global level that things get interesting for you? Or are your interests galactic in scope?

7. **What frustrates the crap out of you, breaks your heart, and makes your blood boil when you look at the world?** Anger, heartbreak and frustration drive creativity and ideas; we're at our best when we're trying to solve problems.

Next steps:

Organise the Post-its into themes. Your answers will form natural groups. What themes have emerged?

1. ....

2. ....

3. ....

4. ....

5. ....

6. ....

7. ....

8. ....

9. ....

10. ....

What are the umbrella themes? Do any of the themes connect and overlap? You may find that some or all sit happily under an umbrella theme. Or maybe one theme resonates more strongly with you right now?

1. ....

2. ....

3. ....

4. ....

5. ....

Can you articulate purpose in a sentence? It may involve you doing something for someone with some kind of result in mind.

My purpose is:

....

....

Chapter 16: Express Your Vision

You are the vision holder and there is no one else who can uphold and cultivate the vision in the same way you can.

— Jenny Sauer Klein

Vision Questions

1. **How do you see your passions and purpose impacting the future?** What change do you want to see as a result of your life's work?

2. **What kind of world do you want to live in?** What does it look like? What are the people like? What is the environment like? How different would it be to how it is today?

3. **What's the craziest idea you've ever had that you've never told anybody about?** The one that keeps popping into your head?

4. **What are you grateful for that you'd love to share with others?** Are you battling a particular challenge? Have you overcome an obstacle that you could help others with? Have you found a solution to a problem you'd like to share with the world? Have you thought of a better way of doing something or making something happen?

5. **It's 2020. What does the world look like?** Humanity? Environment? Community? Describe it in detail.

6. **How is the world different because you existed?** How are other people, animals, or the planet affected by your time here?

Next steps:

Organise the Post-its into themes. Your answers will form natural groups. What themes have emerged?

1. ....

2. ....

3. ....

4. ....

5. ....

6. ....

7. ....

8. ....

9. ....

10. ....

What are the umbrella themes? Do any of the themes connect and overlap?

1. ....

2. ....

3. ....

4. ....

5. ....

Can you articulate your vision in a sentence? It might be a combination of several things that can be expressed in one simple idea. The level of detail is up to you, but the clearer it becomes, the more easily you will be able to express it in a crisp sentence.

My vision is:

....

....

Chapter 17: What Now?

We're coming to the end of the journey, but it's not over yet. Whether you see this as a workbook or a manifesto, its vision is for you to unfurl your brilliance across the universe.

It was my vision to create a kick-ass guide to unfurling your brilliance across the universe and a collection of visionary common sense for life, art and entrepreneurship. It's my hope that the link between these two things is obvious, but if it is not, I have a few more words to say about life, art and entrepreneurship.

Being successful in life is about more than having a great pay check, a house and a car. It's about coming face to face with your most raw, unapologetic self and sharing that with us. It's about having a vision that shares your passion and purpose with your outer world. It's about listening and collaborating with the universe. It's about being *Absolutely on Purpose*.

Being successful in art is about more than having raw talent and the tools of your trade. It's about challenging the furthest edges of your creative genius and exploring in the dark. It's about a passion that glows in that dark and a vision larger than the universe. It's about trust and co-creation with the universe. It's about being *Absolutely on Purpose*.

Being a successful entrepreneur is about more than an 'idea' and venture capital. It's about knowing what you've got that no one else has, and how that can benefit the heart of humanity. It's about an inner calling so strong that forwards is the only direction. It's about changing the story of business and rallying the troops to create a force for social good. It's about being *Absolutely on Purpose*.

Living *Absolutely on Purpose* might be one of the biggest challenges of our time. Will you take the red pill or the blue pill?

I learned this, at least, by my experiment; that if one advances confidently in the direction of his dreams, and endeavours to live the life which he has imagined, he will meet with a success unexpected in common hours. He will put some things behind, will pass an invisible boundary; new, universal, and more liberal laws will begin to establish themselves around and within him; or the old laws will be expanded, and interpreted in his favour in a more liberal sense, and he will live with the license of a higher order of beings ... If you have built castles in the air, your work need not be lost; that is where they should be. Now put the foundations under them.

– Henry David Thoreau, American writer, poet and philosopher

Chapter 18: The Story of *Absolutely on Purpose*

How many hours have you spent at your desk wondering if there was something better you could be doing with your time? How many minutes of every hour do you spend checking social media updates or messaging friends? How many trips do you make to the bathroom / kitchen / corner shop as a way to avoid your current task? How many times have you told yourself that you'll just do one more week / month / year before quitting and following your dream? How often do you gaze out of the window to catch a glimpse of the sky before remembering that you're trapped in a cage of your own making?

Or do you just have that nagging feeling that you're not doing what you're meant to be doing?

I often wonder whether seeing the actual numbers would have shocked me into some kind of realisation, but I was too busy planning my next adventure. I'd breeze through the day anticipating 17.30 (on the dot), salivating like a dog awaiting a bone, astral projecting myself into the future, pretending not to notice the egos and politics that stood between me and perfect poise. I invested all my efforts in creating, educating, inspiring and daydreaming through the mundane. Somehow it wasn't enough. I was missing a *je ne sais quoi*. Could I delete the bits I didn't like?

I wrote this book for you and me as a way to figure out how to delete the bits that we're not passionate about, to connect the parts that give us joy and a sense of purpose, and to create a vision that propels us forward, second by second (and to find a way to do it bravely in the face of the fear of failing miserably).

The best way to become acquainted with a subject is to write a book about it

– Benjamin Disraeli, 1st Earl of Beaconsfield

Back in 2010 I decided I was 'over it'! There had to be a better way. How could I travel forever without exchanging fragments of my soul every other year? My friend told me about Dr John Demartini's seven secret treasures, and I listened with rapture previously unknown to me as my consciousness began to surface: I already had everything I needed to be successful. How could this be?! Then and there I organised a dig for what he calls the buried 'treasure'.

After a few months of digging through the fragments of my past, I found treasure in a blog I had written for six months in 2009, called 'Musings of An Aromastrategist'. Lacking in finesse (understatement: the writing itself was shocking), I savoured the writing process, so within a split second of this discovery I decided to be a writer. From that moment on, my profession was freelance writer, and I wore that hat with the confidence of a Monarch butterfly navigating the distance between the Canadian Rockies to Mexico (in as much as they have never been to their destination but instinctively know where they're going).

The writing skills came afterwards. I enrolled on a five-week online writing course, moved to a remote town in the tropical rainforest of far-north Queensland, Australia, (as one does) and began to cultivate a 'creative space'. Commission after commission, my portfolio grew and another treasure was revealed. Yes, I loved having my name in glossy lifestyle magazines. Yes, I loved getting paid. But the real gem was this: I was sharing my passions and discoveries with others, and this really lit me up.

After that, the dots connected themselves. Everything I'd loved about any role or project dating back to the start of my media career in 2001 involved inspiring and educating others. That is the golden thread. I am a storyteller, good at creating meaning from seemingly random and isolated fragments. I have a natural gift. I have talent! All those hours spent wondering what I could be doing better with my time, and I had actually been doing it all along.

Back in London, my passion for yoga inspired a feature on 'How to choose the right yoga type for you'. I interviewed a handful of yogis and discovered that my favourite part of the entire feature writing process was talking to these 'cool' people. After each interview my skin would tingle, and I would wonder how to get some of that *je ne sais quoi* (Cue: that scene from *When Harry Met Sally*. I think we all want some of that.)

I started another dig to discover the thread that united these inspiring people. They had passion. They had purpose. They had vision. And they reminded me of Bert's character in *Mary Poppins* – the chimney sweep who manifested a vibrant world full of colourful characters by chalking his vision on the pavement. These yogis were painting a vivid picture and walking into it. That was the 'vision' I needed. I dropped my social life, got really clear on how to 'spend' my time, and put pen to paper on my commute, and evenings and weekends.

The result is *Absolutely on Purpose*, a collection of visionary common sense that can be applied to any aspect of life, art or business. I wanted to extract unique insights from these extraordinary beings who had achieved success on their own terms, and to demonstrate what can be achieved both personally and professionally when you're *Absolutely on Purpose*. Yoga philosophy is a liberating and creative lens through which they view the world, and its principles guide the most successful people on the planet (the more you explore yoga as a platform, the more yoga you find in everything).

Absolutely on Purpose is also a celebration of individual brilliance and uniqueness. By bringing together a seemingly homogenous group of people, the project demonstrates how unique our contribution and impact can be when aligned with our passion, purpose and vision, regardless of how many have 'gone before us'.

Yoga, the word, simply means the union of body and mind. It's my belief and experience that when your mind is alive and bright, your body feels the same. When your body is alive and moving, your mind is also active and open. You don't need to have practised yoga to know that, but because many of us don't purposefully and regularly engage in activities that cultivate aliveness and brightness, we are prone to stagnation – physically, mentally, emotionally and spiritually – which blocks us from our highest potential.

The contributors to this book keep their minds and bodies inspired and active, manifesting passion, purpose and vision through their passion for yoga, and in other beautiful ways (for a yogi is never just a yogi). I am, *absolutely on purpose*, sharing this discovery with you in the hope that it will inspire your own dig: to identify *your* passions, define *your* purpose and paint your *own* vibrant, vivid vision. No more options from the assembly line for you, but a wild assortment of treasure to be discovered.

I am certain that amongst these stories, poems and ideas lies buried treasure that will inspire you to dig for your own. Once you've found it, you can share it by unfurling your brilliance across the universe.

Dedication

This book is for you. I love that you have the guts to get naked with your most raw, unapologetic self, and the desire to unfurl your brilliance across the universe.

Just So You Know

I love yoga and have practised irregularly since I discovered a Bikram yoga studio in San Francisco in 2001. Since then I've learned from many teachers and many different styles, each with something to offer me at different points in my journey. There have been times when I've posed every day for weeks, and also months when I've gone without so much as a conscious exhale.

While I have enough knowledge to create my own daily self-practice – and often do – I am definitely not a qualified yoga teacher or an expert on its philosophy. In writing this book I've undertaken research to understand yogic terms and spoken to seasoned yogis. However, traditional yogic philosophy, from something like Patañjali's *Yoga Sūtras* or the *Bhagavad Gita* and their layers of meaning, is beyond my realm of knowledge. These texts beckon a lifetime of study and are the books to study if you're seriously interested in yogic philosophy.

This book is therefore not to be taken as an authority on yogic philosophy, but as a more practical look at how some yogic themes, especially ones that already cross over into popular culture could enhance and enrich our lives on a daily basis. My philosophy is not to be overly serious, but instead to harness profound and universal truths that can help to make sense of *le train-train de la vie quotidienne.**

I've mentioned Escape the City many times. I love the passion and purpose that shines through in their communications, and I invested in the company in October 2011 because I want to support their vision for the business. Like all other references in this book, they are included on a merit basis only.

*The rigmarole of day-to-day life

Resources

Website: http://absolutelyonpurpose.com

Pinterest: pinterest/absolutelyonpur

Facebook Group: https://www.facebook.com/groups/abso-lutelyonpurpose/

Sign up for the newsletter: http://eepurl.com/FNT-P

Must-Read Books:

- *The Element*, by Sir Ken Robertson
- *The Art of Non-Conformity*, by Chris Guillebeau
- *Inspired Destiny*, by Dr John Demartini
- *E-Squared*, by Pam Grout
- *The Muse is In*, by Jill Badonsky
- *An Autobiography*, by M.K. Gandhi
- *Love Yourself*, by Kamal Ravikant
- *The First and Last Freedom*, by Krishnamurti
- *A Return to Love*, by Marianne Williamson
- *Choose Yourself*, by James Altucher
- *Tuesdays with Morrie,* by Mitch Albom

Help Me Spread the Word

This book has been written on a wing and a prayer. Once the idea came to me it had its own unstoppable life force throughout its creation. Developed without traditional publishing support or a marketing budget, it's a love project waiting to be discovered by anyone who wants to live *Absolutely on Purpose*.

If you love it, I'd love you to spread the word about it. I'd like it to get into the hands of those who would benefit from it, whose lives it could enrich, and of those for whom it will create a call to action. I want to get this content out to the people who will use it.

If you love it, you could tell your friends and loved ones about it, or even buy them a copy. You could also tweet and share it. You could even go to amazon to write a review about it.

Thank you for your help sharing *Absolutely on Purpose*.

Acknowledgements

Since your first book is like a baby and it takes a village to raise a child, there are many people without whom this book would never have been able to venture into the world on its own.

I suppose the most strategic thing to do is to go right back to the very beginning...

Thank you to my parents who demonstrated that home is wherever you are at the time, not the bricks and mortar surrounding you. They weren't to know it, but years later this would transform into the realisation that home was within myself; the seed that is planted and nurtured always blooms.

Thank you to Mr Wright at The British School of the Netherlands. You keep the master-disciple relationship going strong. Thank you to Mrs Hickman, Mrs Peacock and Mrs Coleman at Wimbledon High School who had such passion for Latin prose and verse that I now believe anyone can learn anything if passion and purpose are at the helm.

Thank you to Shelley Monrad, founder of Aromaflex, who infused me with such a passion for aromatherapy that I had to start writing about it; this was both a turning point and a stepping stone to revealing all that buried treasure. Essential oils are so integral to my life that I cannot imagine a day without them.

Thank you to Erik Madsen for reading almost every self-help / personal development book on the planet so that I didn't have to; your ability to filter what's needed at any given moment in whatever scenario is incredible.

Thank you to Diana Terrones who read the initial book proposal and gave me some kick-ass advice about the proposition, warning me against up-your-bum-navel-gazing-reflections which, frankly, was a very good tip.

Thank you to the contributors for sharing their wisdom and stories; you have created quite the collection of visionary common sense. Extra thanks to Gaia, Lauren Peterson, Kia Miller, Skye Phillips and Adriana Cortazzo for your help and feedback on the 'yoga stuff'. Extra, extra thanks to Erica Jago, Lauren Peterson, Anne-Marie Newland, Mark Davies, Marc Holzman, Alex Grant, Charlotte Carnegie and Adrianna Cortazzo for your support and encouragement along the way. And finally, thank you to Richard Holroyd, Silla Siebert and Skye Phillips for your absolutely amazing friendship.

Thank you to the brilliant inner circle of beta readers for taking such a hands on role with content editing: Adrian Bonnadio, Adam Bonnadio, Lawrence So, and Annie Dawson-Laforest.

Thank you to an equally amazing second tier of incredible reviewers with a keen, critical eye and awesome encouragement: Ildiko Brunner, Nicola Taylor, Michael Palermo, Snježana Čalo, Gabrielle Gambina, Dorottya Kaba, Fiona Brandt, Adrienn Hanti and Julia Skull.

Thank you to the final reviewers who created time to read the book to ensure it had great support during launch week (in no particular order): Erica Franzen, Adriana Pelosi, Louise Wedgewood, Emily McAuliffe, Deb Parkinson, David Hachez, Emma Murphy, Piers Noller, Lisa Pearson, Rebecca Jones, Laura Knowles, Alanna Michtavy, Karen Kehm, Irina Markovych, Juho Deb, Sophie Bickerdike, Jean-Pierre Levieux, Julia Skull, Tammy Jones, Antonia Thompson, Matt Gill, Ali Jones, David Giltenane, Nicky Hunt, Nicola Stone, Cheryl Mair, Nicola Saltman, Sam Stone, Gregory Schaad-Jackson, Jodie Lewin, Jo Tracey, Krissy Bradfield, Erik Madsen, Jennifer Morton, Mette

Acknowledgements

Børja, Libby Hakim, Tish Dodson, Brooke Lumsden, and Sally Miles.

Thank you to Anna Spargo-Ryan (http://www.annaspargory-an.com) for her excellence in copy-editing; you are a talented woman and I'm so grateful to you for unfurling your brilliance across this manuscript.

Thank you to Loulou Brown (registered at http://www.sfep.org.uk) for her fabulous proofreading. You answered every question with such grace and patience.

Thank you to Carla Buzasi for your clever suggestions and encouragement; they were brilliant and timely.

Thank you to the incredibly talented Jason Botkin (http://www.jasonbotkin.com), who took time out of his own art and the amazing En Masse (http://enmasse.info) to design the wicked, kick-ass book cover. You are a gifted soul with a keen eye and unparalleled aesthetic. I asked for a heart and I got something altogether cosmic. It is gutsy and raw, and I love it.

Thank you to everyone I've ever met and will meet; for I will continue to be the sum of all that I have met.

About the Author

- **Passion:** A pure and rich experience of all that life has to offer and sharing my passions and discoveries with others.

- **Purpose:** To simplify universal truths so they can be integrated into everyday experience.

- **Vision:** The desire within each individual to explore, express and live their own truth.

Photo Credit: Dorottya Kaba

Stephanie Holland is a traveller, writer, aromatherapist and foodie, passionate about life, wellbeing and maximising human potential. A dot connector at heart, she has shared her strategic thinking with small startups like yahoo, msn and AOL, but has gradually realised that she wants to work less and live more. Now her energy is directed towards inspiring heart-centred humans make their imprint, and writing about all the amazing ways we can fire up our body, heart, mind and spirit so that we can live *Absolutely On Purpose*.

She drinks a lot of Earl Grey tea, thinks a lot about coconut macaroons, and loves roses. She currently calls Western Australia home, believing that London will eventually forgive her.

Contact: stephanie@absolutelyonpurpose.com

Website: http://StephanieTHolland.com

Follow: @StephTHolland

Endnotes

1. http://www.kramayoga.com

2. http://yogabeats.com/yogabeats-conflict/

3. http://specialyoga.org.uk

4. http://99u.com

5. http://www.creativitypost.com

6. http://www.huffingtonpost.com/stephen-cope/pur-pose-life_b_1919881.html

7. http://www.marieforleo.com

8. http://www.huffingtonpost.com/stephen-cope/pur-pose-life_b_1919881.html

9. http://www.brandyoga.com

10. http://www.serenityflowsyoga.com/creative-marketing.html

11. Belsky, Scott, 'What Happened to Downtime? The Extinction of Deep Think Sacred Space', Big Think [Accessed: September 2013], http://99u.com/articles/6947/what-happened-to-downtime-the-extinction-of-deep-thinking-sacred-space

12. Orion, Jones, 'How City Living is Changing Human Biology', Big Think [Accessed September 2013], http://bigthink.com/ideafeed/how-city-living-is-changing-human-biology?utm_source=feedburner&utm_medium=feed&utm_campaign=Feed%3A+bigthink%2Fmain+%28Big+Think+Main%29&utm_content=Google+Reader

13. Konnikova, Maria, 'Want to Be Happier and Live Longer? Protect Green Spaces', Scientific American [Accessed: September 2013], http://blogs.scientificamerican.com/lit-

erally-psyched/2013/05/16/want-to-be-happier-and-live-longer-protect-green-spaces/

14. Fehrenbacher, Jill, 'INTERVIEW: Architect James Corner On NYC's High Line Park', Inhabitat [Accessed: September 2013], http://inhabitat.com/interview-architect-james-corner-on-the-design-of-high-line/

15. http://www.allotinabox.com/grow-your-own/

16. http://www.arthermitage.org/Henri-Matisse/Portrait-of-Lydia-Delectorskaya.html

17. 'Elements of Creativity', Iowa State University [Accessed: September 2013], http://www.celt.iastate.edu/creativity/elements.html

18. http://www.fourhourworkweek.com/blog/lifestyle-costing/

19. http://www.openculture.com/freeonlinecourses

20. http://theoreticalminimum.com/home

21. http://yearofprofit.com

22. http://www.escapethecity.org/pages/startup_mba_1

23. http://startuptrainingschool.com

24. http://theleanstartup.com

25. http://m.espn.go.com/general/video?vid=9499560&src=desktop&wjb

26. http://www.upworthy.com/happens-every-time-watching-this-dude-kill-it-on-the-dance-floor-makes-my-heart-burst-open?g=2&c=ufb1

Made in the USA
Lexington, KY
18 February 2014